# INVESTING IN CUBA
## PROBLEMS AND PROSPECT

# Investing in Cuba
## Problems and Prospects

Edited by Jaime Suchlicki
and Antonio Jorge

**Transaction Publishers**
New Brunswick (U.S.A.) and London (U.K.)

175395

0557119

The papers in this volume were presented at the conference, "Investing in Cuba: Problems and Prospects," held in Toronto, Canada, September 8, 1993, which was sponsored by The Research Institute for Cuba, Coral Gables, Florida, and The Canadian Institute of Strategic Studies, Toronto, Canada. The Research Institute for Cuba wishes to thank the Cuban American Research Group (CARG) as well as other private donors for their support.

The **Research Institute for Cuba** (RIC) is an independent Coral Gables, Florida based organization devoted to the study and research of the economic, business, and political trends in contemporary Cuba. In addition to studies and research, the Institute conducts seminars and briefings for the public and private sectors. RIC principals include senior academic researchers, former government officials, and businessmen.

The **Canadian Institute of Strategic Studies'** mandate is to provide a forum to stimulate the research, study, analysis, and discussion of the strategic implications of major national and international issues, events, and trends as they affect Canada and Canadians. Its national and regional seminars are devoted to a variety of topics, attract audiences composed of a wide range of interested persons, and are well reported in the various media.

© 1994  The Research Institute for Cuba, 1453 Miller Road, Coral Gables, Florida 33146.  Published by Transaction Publishers. All rights reserved under International and Pan-American Conventions. No portion of the contents may be reproduced or transmitted in any form, or by any means, electronic or mechanical, including photocopying, recording, or any information storage or retrieval system, without prior permission in writing from the publisher.

**Library of Congress Cataloging-in-Publication Data**

Investing in Cuba: problems and prospects / edited by Jaime Suchlicki, Antonio Jorge.

   p.cm.

"The papers in this volume were presented at the conference, 'Investing in Cuba: Problems and Prospects,' held in Toronto, Canada, September 8, 1993, which was sponsored by The Research Institute for Cuba, Coral Gables, Florida, and The Canadian Institute of Strategic Studies, Toronto, Canada."

ISBN 1-56000-155-0 (cloth); ISBN 1-56000-786-9 (paper)

1. Investments, Foreign — Cuba. 2. Cuba — Economic conditions — 1959-  I. Suchlicki, Jaime. II. Jorge, Antonio. 1931- . III. Research Institute for Cuba  (Coral Gables, Fla.) IV. Canadian Institute of Strategic Studies.
HG5252.I58 1994
332.6'73' 097291 — dc20

94-12389
CIP

Printed in the United States of America.

# CONTENTS

PREFACE
*Alex Morrison* ................................................................ *i*

INTRODUCTION
*Jaime Suchlicki and Antonio Jorge* .............................. *iii*

ETHICAL AND POLITICAL CONSEQUENCES
OF THE AMERICAN EMBARGO OF CUBA
*Irving Louis Horowitz* ................................................. *1*

FOREIGN INVESTMENT OPPORTUNITIES IN CUBA:
EVALUATING THE RISKS
*Antonio Jorge and Robert David Cruz* ...................... *17*

CREDITORS' RIGHTS:
CLAIMS AGAINST CUBAN CONFISCATED ASSETS
*Robert C. Helander* ................................................... *37*

INVESTING IN CUBA: A PERSONAL VIEW
*Otto J. Reich* ............................................................. *51*

BUSINESS PERSPECTIVE ON INVESTMENTS IN CUBA
*Alberto Luzarraga* ..................................................... *63*

THE REALITIES OF INVESTING IN CUBA
*Donald McQ. Shaver, Jr.* ........................................... *69*

CANADA-CUBA TRADE RELATIONS:
PROBLEMS AND PROSPECTS
*Allan Gotlieb* ............................................................ *77*

THE EXPERIENCE OF EASTERN EUROPE:
SEVEN LESSONS FOR CUBA
*Vendulka Kubalkova* ................................................. *91*

APPENDIX I
Cuban Foreign Investment Law ................................ *115*

APPENDIX II
Current Investments in Cuba .................................... *172*

0557119

~~175395~~

# PREFACE

The Canadian Institute of Strategic Studies (CISS) is grateful to have hosted the seminar, "Investing in Cuba: Problems and Prospects," with The Research Institute for Cuba (RIC), which is well-known for its scholarly activities with regard to all aspects of Cuban affairs.

Canada and America have pursued two different courses of action with regard to relations with Cuba. The Canadian approach has been to continue diplomatic and trade ties, while the Americans have steadfastly refused to do so. Now that the Cuban government has indicated that it is loosening some of the strictures that have been in place for decades, it will be interesting to observe the American reaction.

The collection of edited papers in this volume were originally presented at the seminar, and their authors were chosen to represent a wide range of views.

*Alex Morrison*
*Executive Director*
*The Canadian Institute of Strategic Studies*

# INTRODUCTION

Jaime Suchlicki and Antonio Jorge, editors

Since the last century foreign investment has been growing in importance throughout the world economic scene. The expansion of investments that cross geographical boundaries is directly related to the acceleration of growth in the western world and among Third World countries as developing economies. In effect, the latter have erupted into the world economic system no longer as colonial territories but generally as candidates for investment funds and economic aid as they seek to follow the path of the developed economies.

Capital resources, however, are extremely scarce relative to the needs and aspirations of the world's economies. Most of the capital investment, direct or indirect, short or long term, finds its way to the rich countries of the world. By far, these are the destinations of choice for the capital flows circulating in the international economic system. This, of course, makes sense. Among the driving forces behind capital movements, the most important are safety and rate of return. Liquidity and flexibility, along with the presence of alternative opportunities, are also considerations of prime importance. Obviously, the capital and money markets of affluent countries, the strength and variety of their financial institutions and organizations, ranging from stock markets to money and investment funds, their public investments like treasury bills or municipal bonds, and their private ones like corporate

Jaime Suchlicki, is professor of history and international studies at the University of Miami. He is editor of *North-South Magazine* and the *Journal of Interamerican Studies and World Affairs*.

Antonio Jorge is professor of economics and international relations, Florida International University, Miami.

commercial paper, have no remote parallel in less developed nations.

The combination of stability and low political risk, a relatively attractive rate of return, and the abundance of worthwhile investment opportunities is an unbeatable one for governments and private investors in search of a haven for their funds. Most of the time this combination is found only in the wealthy countries.

Capital flows to less developed countries are, therefore, restricted as to volume and also exhibit a high degree of instability. Not only do capital resources going to those countries represent a relatively small percentage of the total, but the amount itself fluctuates widely in response to political or economic disturbances.

The task of attracting investments to developed countries is extremely competitive. These countries do not simply receive capital resources in proportion to their needs or their desire to host foreign investments. Funds are channeled to those markets in response to the existence of real economic opportunities in them.

In turn, those opportunities are dependent upon a very broad range of social, political, and economic elements. For one, political instability and latent social disturbances are ever present risks in a large number of poor countries. The premium to compensate for the economic disasters occurring in the wake of political uprisings must, indeed, oftentimes be very great. This naturally diminishes the number of projects worthy of consideration under those circumstances.

But how many such extremely high yielding activities awaiting investment are there in many of those societies? Not many if we are to judge by Adam Smith's limiting factor in the application of the principle of division of labor, namely, the extent of the market. The more underdeveloped a country is, the smaller its market; that is, the less the actual purchasing power or effective demand of the population there is. That is what makes single investments or even a cluster of investments frequently so ineffective in poor countries. An investment wave below the critical minimum effort threshold will not succeed because there is not enough real income to go around to absorb the output of the new projects. The lower the population's per capita income and the smaller the available surplus over and above current consumption and depreciation investment levels, the riskier the investment is.

Aside from the dangers surrounding an investment due to

sociopolitical and market limitation type deterrents, there are others stemming from the inadequate socioeconomic infrastructure characterizing most less developed countries. The more underdeveloped a nation is, the more deficient its infrastructure-related services are. Naturally, this is directly connected to the insufficiency of investment, which is proportional to the economic and social deficiencies of a nation. All of this contributes to the creation of the vicious circle of poverty. In the end, a country is poor because it is poor, and as an extension, there is not sufficient investment at present because of inadequate investment in the past.

One other point is the instability inherent in underdeveloped countries themselves. The lopsidedness, openness, and fragility of the production matrix of underdeveloped countries, along with the particular susceptibility of primary goods and agricultural commodities to sharp and erratic price fluctuations in the world market, predisposes those countries' economies to violent ups and downs in tandem with the fluctuations of the world economy.

Clearly, the tendency toward macroeconomic disequilibria infringes unfavorably upon the economy of a less developed country with far more force than it would upon the economy of a developed country. This means that over and above the risk calculations for a particular investment and for the macro environment in which it takes place, one would have to add those other risks deriving from changes in the world economy. The latter kinds of risks deeply affect every investment, even those unrelated to the foreign sector of the economy.

It is well-known how nightmarish dealing with the bureaucracy of a less developed country can be. If, additionally, that bureaucracy claims to be of a Marxist-Leninist ideological persuasion, the imbroglio can become even more complicated. The red tape that is characteristic of the civil service of underdeveloped countries waxes exponentially once central planning and administration are added to it. These extra levels of bureaucracy would inevitably raise the cost of any investment. Delays, regulations, interferences, bureaucratic permits, and limitations on decision making all conspire to detract from the efficiency of an economic operation, reducing the net rate of return considerably, relative to what it could have been under less onerous conditions.

High among the hindrances to investment in less developed countries, but most particularly in the case of socialist societies, is the problem of economic irrationality. The more imperfect markets and prices are, the more inefficient an economic activity turns out to be. The epitome of such a situation is found in centrally planned economic systems. The accounting or administrative prices of planners are essentially irrational because of their incapability to reflect the scarcity value of economic resources. Therefore, the process of resource allocation, which constitutes the very crux of economic efficiency, is irremediably flawed.

These considerations explain what to many has proved to be an unsolvable puzzle: namely, the disastrous level of inefficiency of socialist firms and enterprises, despite the vast investment effort undertaken by socialist states and their avowed preference for advanced techniques and capital-intensive methods of production. Most of the production plants in those societies are woefully inadequate and would have to be scrapped if subjected to the discipline of competition under a free trade regime. In this same context, it is interesting to note that former socialist countries faced enormous difficulties due to their lack of competitiveness in exporting manufactured goods to markets in western countries.

Cuba has the appearance of offering significant opportunities for investment. It is the largest island in the Caribbean, with a population of over 11 million; it is close to the United States, which should provide a large and prosperous market; it has a well-educated and trained population; and it suffers from a great need for material goods and for the rebuilding of its deteriorating infrastructure. Also, as the Castro era draws to an end and U.S.-Cuban relations eventually are normalized, tourism, mining, agriculture, and construction will become significant targets for foreign investment.

And yet, in reality Cuba combines the worst features of underdeveloped and socialist societies. Cuba typifies those characteristics mentioned as being intimately associated with the condition of underdevelopment. It probably is the most inefficient among the former socialist nations. By far, it is also the poorest in terms of per capita income. It follows, therefore, that all the drawbacks and disadvantages that have been described as related to attempts at investing in less developed and socialist countries apply with special emphasis to the Cuban case. Cuba, in other words, combines the worst of both worlds as far as investment opportunities are concerned.

Moreover, Cuba's economic decline in the last five years has reached catastrophic proportions, with no end in sight for the deflationary spiral. The entropy of the Cuban economy as it keeps on contracting, because of the asphyxiating lack of indispensable imports, has no parallel in recent history, perhaps with the exception of the Cambodian experience under the Khmer Rouge.

Cuba's extreme dependence on foreign trade and the adaptation of its economy for nearly three decades to an unnatural and immense subsidy inflow, which created an artificial economy that has now disappeared, paradoxically has proved to be its own nemesis. Cuba does not have a viable economy of its own. As nearly every category of inputs keeps on decreasing from one period to the next, so the spiraling vicious circle of pauperization keeps on descending unremittingly.

In Cuba there is no internal market to speak of. Consumption is limited by a strict and severe rationing regime. Whatever transactions take place outside it are in the illegal black market, which operates with scarce dollars and stolen merchandise. Meanwhile, the Cuban peso continues to depreciate as its purchasing power becomes nil and its function as a means of exchange approximates the vanishing point. This process is being accelerated by a huge and persistent governmental budgetary deficit and the virtual absence of any stabilizing fiscal and monetary policies. Under such extreme conditions and with no foreign exchange reserves, convertability is totally out of the question.

Sugar production, Cuba's mainstay export, has reached levels comparable to that of the Great Depression period, while the prices of other supplementary primary commodities continue their downward trend in the international market.

Efforts at diversifying production both for domestic and export purposes have proved to be notorious failures, despite enormous amounts of misplaced investment. Furthermore, the economic and social infrastructures of the nation are not only in a state of disrepair but are actually collapsing. The outdated electric grid cannot supply the meager needs of consumers and industry, transportation services have almost vanished, communication facilities are totally obsolete, and sanitary and medical services have deteriorated so badly that contagious diseases of epidemic proportions constitute a real menace to the population.

Under these present conditions it would be risky, if not foolhardy, to invest in Cuba. Even the export sectors, like tourism, which seem to be relatively prosperous and immune to the economy's malady, will eventually fall victim to the general poverty of the country. It is impossible for isolated sectors of enclaves of economic activity to survive indefinitely under such cataclysmic conditions.

One other point of extreme importance to consider when evaluating the economic wisdom of investing in Cuba under Castro is that of the general subsidization of economic activities. The extremely lax fiscal, tariff, and labor policies now in force are likely to be rapidly replaced by more economically rational ones as soon as the Castro regime is supplanted. The present policies can only be understood as the desperate actions of a political system in urgent need of short-term financial resources in order to retain its grip on power.

Related to the preceding point is the crucial issue of the structural changes that will eventually take place in the price system as Cuba inevitably undergoes its transformation from a centrally planned and administered economy into a market-based one. At that time, a revolutionary mutation will take place in the cost accounting and price practices and calculations of business enterprises. There is no way now for an investor to anticipate the impact of such reforms on supply and demand conditions, and thus on the market position, solvency, and profit-making potential of his economic enterprise. The East European experience is a prime example of the enormous difficulty involved in salvaging apparently healthy enterprises once a change of economic system has taken place.

There is also a veritable maze of legal problems posed by the issue of the legality of foreign investments and the validity of property rights acquired during the Castro era once it comes to an end. Obviously, both Cuban nationals and foreigners whose properties were confiscated during the early years of the revolution will reclaim them as soon as this become feasible. The United States, as well as other countries whose citizens' assets were seized without adequate compensation, stand ready to support their nationals' claims. Additionally, Cubans living in different parts of the world eagerly await the opportunity of exercising their legal rights before the Cuban courts in a post-Castro situation. Again, the East European example is a good indication of the complexities, delays, and uncertainties accompanying the reclamation process.

A different kind of problem is that posed by the legality of investments and the legitimacy of property rights relating to assets and facilities that did not exist before the Castro regime acceded to power. This, indeed, is an extremely sensitive and technically convoluted issue. It should be noted that exaggerated popular sentiments and a politically incendiary rhetoric will certainly await those who are now investing in Cuba. At the very least, they should expect to deal with a conflictive social climate and an adverse business environment. That is, at this time investors will invariably encounter an ambience in Cuba that is not conducive to productive operations.

As for the purely legal matter of the status of investment projects and contractual obligations entered into during Castro's tenure of power, there is no dearth of scholarly opinions questioning their validity before a court of law. Under the precepts of international law, agreements subscribed to by usurping authorities and/or others that are clearly harmful and detrimental to the public good or common wealth, or which violate the civil rights of the population (such as the case of forced or coerced labor), are considered null and void.

None of the above addresses a fundamental issue of extraordinary moral impact: lending assistance to a totalitarian regime that cruelly and callously has systematically violated the most elementary human rights of the population of a nation. The Cuban regime stands condemned by the United Nations as one among the few throughout the world that share that notoriety.

If investment and trade embargoes imposed in the past on those political systems that have been convicted of heinous crimes and abominable deeds against their populations have any sense and can claim to be morally justified, the case of Cuba must be among the most salient ones, symbolizing a country whose population has been uninterruptedly governed by a totalitarian regime for thirty-five years.

It is to be hoped that investors and entrepreneurs, cognizant of the drama of the Cuban people, will realize their ethical and moral obligations and abstain from lending success to a regime that will be harshly judged by history as well as by those who have been victimized by it.

*Jaime Suchlicki*
*Antonio Jorge*
*Coral Gables, Florida*
*May 1994*

# ETHICAL AND POLITICAL CONSEQUENCES OF THE AMERICAN EMBARGO OF CUBA

Irving Louis Horowitz

The purpose of this study is to provide a game theoretical framework for the analysis of current political and ethical issues involved in a reconsideration of American foreign policy toward Cuba. It is clear that while few celebrate the character or structure of the Castro regime, a debate is emerging as to the policy toward the regime in light of Castro's continuing staying power.

Political issues turn, therefore, not so much upon different appraisals but changing policies toward Cuba. Ethical issues turn on what policies are best calculated to cause the people of Cuba the least grief or despair without giving sustenance to the dictatorship. In this multi-layered situation, policy making becomes freighted with extrinsic considerations that make this a special moment in the nearly thirty-five-year history of Castro's Cuba.

This paper reviews the arguments currently being put forth for a lifting or a continuation of the embargo and also asks whether the embargo is intended to be an effective economic mechanism or a symbolic statement of United States foreign policy. The position taken is that demands for policy change are being made without clear regard for what, if any, fundamental changes are taking place in the Castro regime.

Irving Louis Horowitz is Hannah Arendt distinguished professor of sociology and political science at Rutgers University. Among his writings on Latin America are *Masses in Latin America; Cuban Communism,* now entering its eighth edition; and, most recently, *The Conscience of Worms and the Cowardice of Lions,* delivered as the Bacardi Lectures for 1992.

The analysis concludes with a reaffirmation of the causal sequence outlined by present and past American administrations: first, democracy; second, elections; third, policy alteration and reconsideration. These can occur in rapid succession and almost simultaneously. But in an environment where one "side" is rigid, the prospects for flexibility on the other "side" are limited. Thus, one can expect a moderate tactical thaw in relationships but little in the way of immediate basic policy shifts.

## The Significance of Embargoes

To start with, we require an appreciation that an embargo is a policy designed to achieve certain ends. It is not an act to be taken lightly. Nor is it an act undertaken by friendly nations in dispute. An embargo represents a termination, in whole or in part, of goods and services by one nation to a second nation deemed hostile and demonstrably unfriendly. An embargo, however, is a far cry from an act of war or invasion of the territory of another nation. Nor does it represent the cessation of all contact between the hostile nations. As in politics generally, an embargo has both real consequences and symbolic significance.

The act of embargoing is very much part of a game theoretical environment: 1) it involves a situation in which two or more nations or individuals are involved; 2) it involves a decision in pursuit of the objectives of at least one player; 3) it involves a decision-making scenario of one option over others that may be available; 4) it involves an expected utility payoff, that is, the success of a policy; and finally, 5) its aim is to change the political behavior of the opponent, or failing that, to effect the removal of the opponent in favor of a different player, one who is more interested in a new consensus rather a continuation of the conflict.[1]

## The U.S. Embargo of Cuba

The American embargo of Cuba, which reached its apex in *The Cuba Democracy Act of 1992,* is as powerful and forthright an example of the above description of the game theoretical environment as any currently practiced by the United States. Clearly, as the testimony and discussion have made evident, this has been a contentious policy.[2] Its consecration in law took place rather late in the policy game, so that the de jure policy came considerably after the de facto state of conflict that exists between the United States and Cuba. To further complicate matters, and in our rhetoric at least, the players changed with the election of William Clinton, a Democrat, replacing George Bush, a Republican. This signaled a potential for change in policy approaches.

It should be added that on the other side, the key player, Fidel Castro, continues as Cuba's leader, entering his thirty-fifth year in power, and clearly is an individual with a staying power far in excess of the expectations of his critics worldwide. And while Castro modestly welcomed the change of players in the United States, to date no substantial change in Cuba's internal policies, leading to the imposition of the embargo to begin with, have taken place. For example, there have been only slight shifts toward a market or free economy, no lessening of control of the police and armed forces in the everyday domination of Cuba, and no movement toward popular elections or a multiparty system, each of which might be taken as signs that the initial decision to impose the embargo would be subject to review.

Hence, such a discussion is less a matter of studying changes in the structure of Cuban domestic or foreign policy, although these are underway, but more, whether the embargo works, the political question, and also whether it is a "good," the ethical question. That is to say, the discussion over the American embargo takes place during a time in which the behavior of the "other side," Cuba, is essentially a constant. This is a debate not on the political efficacy or personal decency of Fidel Castro, as it is uniformly understood that his days are numbered and the worth of his regime permanently tarnished by authoritarian practices.[3] Rather, this debate is on the best ways of ridding the Cuban island of Castro and assisting its people in the process. I shall now turn toward just such considerations.

The great victory of what can be termed the orthodox position, the one held by the Cuban American National Foundation, was the signing into law of the *Cuba Democracy Act*. In one fell swoop, this piece of legislation tightened the United States' embargo and held out the promise of a loosened communications framework. However, by virtue of its strong linkages to both the Reagan and Bush administrations, the Cuban American National Foundation has lost a substantial degree of its insider cachet. But not entirely. It was strong enough to void the appointment of Mario Baeza as assistant secretary of state for

Inter-American Affairs, and it was also a powerful force in the continuation of support for Radio Martí, although this umbrella did not extend to Television Martí. The House Appropriations Committee refused to authorize funds for the station's broadcasts to Cuba, and it is clear that the White House made scant efforts to overturn congressional decision making.

## Reconsideration of the Embargo

On the other side, a plethora of organizations have emerged to urge some form of reconciliation between the United States and Cuba. These include groups such as *Cambio Cubano*, headed by Eloy Gutierrez Menoyo, and various socialist parties such as the *Cuban Democratic Party* and the *Christian Democratic Party*. The position taken by these rather feeble groups is essentially that with the collapse of the Soviet empire, Cuba is not an international threat, and with the loss of revenues from sugar and tobacco crops, Cuba is not much of a hemispheric threat either. They are hoping for a cancellation, in part or in full, of the embargo. Such a view is described by former Ambassador Wayne Smith as "A Pragmatic Cuba Policy."[4] At the least, these domestic support groups expect the United States to condemn any illegal activities emanating from this country, such as the May 1993 effort by Alpha 66 to deliver automatic rifles and explosives to Cuba from American shores, or the hijacking of air craft. But it should be kept in mind that the Bush administration also adhered to a position of strict non-intervention into the internal affairs of Cuba.[5]

The debate is far less one of ideology than strategy. For example, two people, strongly identified with conservative politics in general, and quite specifically on Cuban affairs, William Ratliff and Roger Fontaine, have urged a deep reconsideration of the embargo policy. The importance of this break in conservative ranks warrants a direct quotation from their op-ed piece:

> Clinton must facilitate the exchange of people and ideas. Yes, exiles and others who visit Cuba will take in some foreign currency. But despite Castro's efforts to segregate them with his own form of tourist apartheid, their presence, and the news they bring with them, will testify to the superiority of democratic free market economics over

Fidel's despotic socialism. The end of the embargo and these exchanges will show that the United States is not hostile to Cubans in general, and they will stimulate the growth of alternatives in Cuba's stunted civil society. U.S. policy must show that Castro's warning of 'après Fidel, le déluge' is self-serving propaganda.[6]

The influential Gannett flagship paper, *USA Today,* has also called for a changing of political course. Its editorial argues, "Cuba shouldn't get tougher penalties than Chile or Brazil, enriched by U.S. aid despite rights violations, or China, which enjoys normal U.S. trade despite Tiananmen Square." The editorial adds that the embargo has worn thin in the international community, and besides, "Lifting the embargo makes economic sense. It would reap for the U.S.A. about $223 million of the annual trade now flowing to Europeans entering the Cuban banking and tourist markets."[7] Such influential Cubanologists as Jorge Dominguez have echoed and amplified such sentiments regarding lifting the embargo: "Doing something like this would be a bold political risk in the American context but would produce a Cuba very different from anything we have ever seen: something that looks and feels like a market economy."[8]

It is evident that Castro has understood the importance of this sea change in Cuban American and non-Cuban American thinking. He has taken three admittedly small measures to improve relations: a willingness to discuss U.S. property embargoes in the early 1960s — now worth roughly $6 billion; a reduction in the size of the swollen Cuban armed forces; and the use of dollars in tourist stores. Of course, the problem with these concessions is that Cuba is a country on the verge of bankruptcy with hardly any cash reserves. Thus, even if Castro admits to obligations, they are not likely to be fulfilled. And by the same token, the diminution of the military is a function of a country in which shortages are enormous, and the ability to reward the military no longer exists. In any event, it might well be argued that a reduced military is a reduced threat to Castro's personal rule. The Ochoa affair is, after all, only five years old and remains etched in the minds of those who might contemplate a *golpe de estado* from above. The infusion of a dollar economy carries the risk of separating the small elites from the masses of Cubans living on substandard wages. Such hard currency stores hardly helped Eastern European communism, and their potential for helping the economy of Cuba is not much better.

## *Responses to the Aperture*

The responses to the new aperture have not been long in coming. Perhaps the most typical of the orthodox views is by dynamic Republican member of the U.S. House of Representatives, Ileana Ros-Lehtinen. Essentially, her position is that the United States ". . . should not betray Cubans now by letting Castro get what he needs to keep his regime afloat." She adds, ". . . deprived of Soviet subsidies, Castro no longer has the oil to power his tanks, he no longer has the power to run his searchlights, and he no longer can buy the very goods that he denies to the Cuban people. What is needed now is a clear focus on the ultimate prize of a free Cuba and not to allow an aging dictator to further delay the advent of democracy."[9]

And mainline conservatives' voices have also begun to speak out on the question of lifting the embargo. The position of syndicated columnist John J. Farmer is rather typical:

> How will Fidel's finish occur? One hopes not as violently as Nicolae Ceausescu. But like the Romanian tyrant's, his will probably be an inside job, too, either by military coup or popular [up]rising or some combination thereof. But just as there is no reason for the West to help Castro, there is even less to take a violent hand in hurrying him into history. He is not even a minor menace anymore. It is best to let the Cubans decide when they have had their fill of Fidel.[10]

Here then, we have an outline of positions on an American debate on Castro's Cuba nearly thirty-five years after the assumption of power. This is hardly a world shattering debate, but it does serve as a benchmark for the Clinton administration and its foreign policy. Curiously, early examples of Democratic administration responses have been extremely careful. Essentially, it is a cause-effect sequence that is at stake:

•If there are free and untrammeled elections, then the embargo will be removed.

•If there is restoration of an internationally recognized human rights policy, then there can be a withdrawal from Guantánamo.

•If free market rights are established, then negotiations can be undertaken for new trade and aid.

This cause and effect sequence is clearly within the rights of a big power and enforceable due to the repressibilities of a small power. President Clinton has demonstrated an adroit ability to play power politics on a global canvas. His position also reveals an acute sense of domestic pressures and counter-pressures.[11]

Signals, however, from the Clinton administration have been mixed: a passive executive permitting an activist legislature to cut Television Martí from the United States Information Agency and substantial reduction in the budget of Radio Martí. However, the administration has also moved to cut telephonic transmission from the United States to Cuba via Canada, once Castro made it his policy to curtail sharply direct telephonic communication. Prosecutors in the U.S. Attorney's Office have drafted a proposed indictment charging the Cuban government with being a racketeering and drug dealing enterprise.[12] Thus far, such an indictment has not been issued — whether for lack of hard evidence or political caution is hard to determine.

On the Cuban side, too, there is ambivalence: reopening direct forwarding of monies and goods from Miami to Havana has been proposed but not implemented, on the ever-present humanitarian grounds. In the larger picture, private-sector initiatives — sometimes legalized, other times not sanctioned — have sprung up. At the same time, Sunday drills against the coming mythic invasion from the United States continue to be held.[8] So an uneasy truce remains in place. The initiatives have been shifting from "hawkish" to "dovish" impulses, initiated by people like former Ambassador Wayne Smith, Washington's senior diplomat in Havana from 1979 to 1982, and a cluster of retired army and navy officers visiting Cuba with the ostensible purpose of "easing tensions," which translates into some sort of higher profile recognition for the Castro regime.[13]

## Clinton Administration Sends Mixed Signals

We come now to the policy recommendations toward Cuba that have been offered in the fulcrum of a new American administration. The installation of a new administration in Washington does indeed propel the idea of a different set of relations between Castro's Cuba and the United States. Talk has already begun to the effect that after a respectful period of time, the Clinton administration might seek the path of reconciliation with Fidel's dictatorship. For the moment, the administration's public signals are mixed: sanctioned, but informal, trade missions to Cuba; proposed total withdrawal of funds from the North-South Center; putting a career officer without an ideological commitment to the exile community in charge of the Latin American desk at the Department of State; yet leaving funds intact for Radio and Television Martí, this at a time when there is a decision to dismantle Radio Free Europe and Radio Liberty.

There are those who would counsel renewed effort at reconciliation and accommodation between the Castro regime and the United States. The argument essentially proceeds as follows: 1) the diplomatic isolation of Cuba serves no useful foreign policy end; 2) with a new administration in Washington, the United States has the opportunity to wipe the slate clean; and, consequently, 3) such a restoration of economic and political relations would signal the eventual democratization of Cuba. To be sure, there are variations on this scenario, depending on the audiences whose support is solicited. Hard-liners are told that such an *aperture* would hasten the departure of Castro from power, while liberals are encouraged to believe that this opening would encourage a renewed human rights posture on the part of the communist officials in Havana. In its remarkable and singular assault on a piece of U.S. congressional legislation, *The Cuba Democracy Act of 1992*, the United Nations General Assembly has already signaled its desire for a policy shift to a softer line on the part of the United States. And recent statements by Castro indicate that he sees repudiation of this piece of legislation as a central goal of his government's foreign policy.

The problem with the drumbeat for policy change inheres in the assumptions being made: above all, the assumption that the fault in present United States relations with Castro's Cuba is uniquely that of the former; similarly, the ideas that Castro's intentions were badly misunderstood to start with and that given an opportunity to mend his ways, Castro would become an excellent hemispheric citizen seem strained. Finally, there is the suggestion that with the collapse of the Soviet empire, communist Cuba is a minor irritant, one that a benevolent world power such as the United States can readily afford to treat in a benign rather than punitive manner.

Those who argue for reconciliation have been heard fully and fairly. Indeed, such advocates have been given a better hearing than they usually grant those who stand in firm opposition to such a turn. What is wrong with such an argument for benevolence?

## Accommodating Castro: Inconsistent With U.S. Policy

To start with, a policy of accommodation with the Castro government is not consistent with United States policy toward tyrannies. For the United States to stand on moral principle when it comes to "friendly tyrants" in the Middle East or Asia, but to embrace Castro on pragmatic grounds would be a curious turn. It would grant Castro the fruits of his aggression, providing him with diplomatic succor the United States has accorded neither to Kim Il Sung of North Korea nor to Saddam Hussein of Iraq.

Such a policy would also deny the realities of thirty-four years of implacable opposition by Castro to any and every democratic regime in the Western Hemisphere. As Abraham Lowenthal noted in a recent review of Latin America in *Foreign Affairs*, democratic regimes in Latin America are far shakier than one round of popular elections admits to.[14] Such a policy turn would hold Castro blameless for adventures in Angola that did nothing to insure the democratization of that nation, and de facto would legitimate his principle of military intervention by an armed praetorian force throughout the world. The enthusiasm with which Castro and his revolution have been supported by ultra-radical elements in the United States has had less to do with the terrible loss of lives and destabilization of democratic regimes inspired by Cuba than with Castro's posture of anti-Americanism, a posture that continues to link the enemies of freedom the world over.

There is also the simple reality that such overtures have rarely been effective in modern diplomacy. The capitulation of Neville Chamberlain at Munich did not insure peace in his time but only hastened the hard-hearted march of Adolf Hitler through the whole of Europe. The Molotov-von-Ribbentrop non-aggression pact between Germany and Russia did not forestall or terminate the forces of aggression or even buy very much time for Russia to arm. It simply hastened that dark day in June 1941 when Hitler extended the war to Russia. On the other hand, it must be acknowledged that Nixon's opening to China did have positive consequences, although as we saw with Tiananmen Square, this opening did not so much insure democracy in China as it encouraged economic stability in that country.

Clearly, there is a serious question as to whether a softening toward Castro might weaken democratic elements throughout the Caribbean region, especially in shaky places like Nicaragua, Haiti, and El Salvador. If it did, for this reason alone, it would become an extremely risky proposal.

Some might object that analogies of Castro with Hitler, Stalin, or Mao are inherently fallacious, that Castro is not remotely capable of such exercises of world or regional power. That may well be true, but hardly as a result of the soft-liners. Castro's record of thirty-four years of implacable opposition to democratic norms, indeed, his continuing assaults within Cuba against the smallest signs of opposition indicate that the analogy of one police state to another is quite appropriate. And one must still reckon with a bloated Cuban armed force entirely capable of regional troublemaking should the occasion arise. The argument that Castro is now powerless and, hence, need not be opposed subverts any claims to moral superiority for Western democratic forces. If one argues that American policy making should only act against tyrants when there is potential for naked aggression and the United States is directly threatened, there is no room for action when democratic institutions are threatened, whether by big or small totalitarian states.

## Rethinking American Policy

There is, nonetheless, a need to rethink the basis of current American policy toward Castro's Cuba. For much of our policy has indeed been based on premises that are in need of sharp revision in the light of the collapse of the Soviet empire. Such a policy revision may not necessarily comfort the friends of democracy. Indeed, behind so-called efforts to "normalize" relations between the United States and the present-day rulers of Cuba lies an effort, sometimes conscious, but mostly unconscious, to deny the totalitarian character of today's Cuba.

There is a remarkable congruence of opinion from eye-witness sources on the economic collapse of Cuban communism. The work of Spencer Reiss in *Newsweek*, Tim Golden and Jo Thomas in *The New York Times*, Andres Oppenheimer in *The Miami Herald*, John Newhouse in *The New Yorker*, and Anne-Marie O'Connor in *Esquire* underscore the remarkable ability of on-site observers to see better and further than the social scientists turned Castrologists that I reviewed in *The Conscience of Worms and the Cowardice of Lions.*[15] There is little purpose in repeating what this sextet of reporters have so forcefully and brilliantly written in their accounts of present day Cuba. But one should examine the significant meanings shared by these commentaries for the light they shed on the fundamental theory and practice of international relations.

The collective journalistic portrait yields five interrelated propositions:

1. There is a virtually irreversible revolution of fallen expectations in Cuba.

2. There is a movement from development to underdevelopment in slow stages.

3. For most Cubans, non-participation rather than direct opposition has become a buffer against the worst infections of the regime.

4. Cuba has become a land without hope, but without the tools or infrastructure for rebellion.

5. Emigration as a safety valve for Castro, or as a mechanism to avoid protest, has just about dried up.

The relative weight of these elements can be challenged, but not their presence in the Cuban mosaic of 1993.

The famous formula for a revolution of rising (or falling) expectations must now be modified to take into account the situation in Cuba, where the revolution of fallen expectations is evident. When a society converts from automobiles to oxen; when capitalist evils return in an enhanced form as socialist virtues, specifically as class division, prostitution, foreign tourism (already twice that of 1958, the last year prior to Castro's golpe); and when a society literally goes from light to darkness, then elimination of the extremes of social stratification which the Cuban Revolution sought to alleviate, if not entirely overthrow, are fast being restored.

## How Will It End?

Castro has insured himself a unique position of power by clever, indeed brilliant, dismemberment of all sources of opposition, from the bureaucracy to the military. What he cannot insure himself against are the ravages of time and biological fate. The revenge of nature, not politics, may ultimately overcome the dictator. Whether it is a political or direct mass struggle, an assassin's bullet, or a palace coup d'état, the regime will come to termination. The question is only how it will end.

Even if elements of the social and political process conspire to permit one or two more years of grace, Castro must still face the unbending will of time itself. History may not absolve Fidel, but biology surely will not overlook him. He may survive one more mistake, one more tactical blunder, one more episode of forgetfulness, but the dictator will fall. And on that judgment day, those who stood firm against this long night of tyranny will be able to relent, to relax, and some will return. Some envision a transfer of power from Castro to a younger individual or cohort, but this supposes a transfer of charisma as well.

Undoubtedly, Castro has benefited from the unique circumstances that permitted more than a million of Cuba's best and brightest to emigrate to the United States. This may also have been a bonanza for the United States, for the talents and creativities of the Cuban people had made their country one of the region's most innovative. But the emigration also permitted Castro to rid himself of a permanent base of opposition in class and occupational terms, if not direct military opposition. It is simply hard to believe that Castro would have long survived in the absence of such a mass migration.

On the other hand, it is equally difficult to imagine a firm United States policy toward Castro without a Cuban exile community. We tend to emphasize, sotto voce to be sure, the costs of the exile community to the advancement of democratic norms within Cuba. But it must be said that the Cuban communities of Miami, parts of New Jersey, and elsewhere, have done something easily overlooked: They have provided a spiritual and at times material haven for people in similar dire straits from other places. The Nicaraguan exile community in Miami readily became part of the Latino influence and was permitted a base of opposition to the Sandinistas — one that met with considerable success.

It has sometimes been said that democracy flourishes in small states. While this may be the case, it is also correct to point out that dictatorship may also flourish in small states; Cambodia, Haiti, and North Korea come readily to mind. In the case of Cuba, control has been ironclad because of the ease with which surveillance is possible, movement of citizens monitored, and opposition thwarted in early stages. Cuba is not simply a small state, but an island state, and this increases a potential for isolation that is clearly far beyond anything feasible in Eastern Europe in the past or the Far East in the present. We have become so enamored of political and/or economic determinism that even the rudiments of geographic variables have been lost to our generation.

But all these points have been made by others as well as myself in the past. The fact remains that while *conditions* for revolution in Cuba are extant, the *capacities* for revolution are not. In part, this is simply a function of Fidel's perfection of the tools of tyranny. This is also a reflection that revolutions of falling expectations are as real as revolutions of rising expectations. Survival is quite possible in a lower order of economic well being. The Cuban regime no longer makes participation mandatory, so that non-political life or, better, depolitization, is taking place on a massive scale. Nor should it be forgotten that while the rest of Latin America may have spurned the Castro road to domination, many still maintain cordial diplomatic relations and provide a framework for regime legitimation that was absent in Eastern Europe.

Castro will fall as surely as his regime has failed in its purposes. Indeed, he himself now speaks of being out of power in five years. Of course, he means by that a removal of his person from power but not dismemberment of the Communist Party of Cuba. So the struggle has shifted from personal rule to regime continuation. Castro knows as much. It is a sobering thought that so many predictions of Castro's failure and collapse — from Fulgencio Batista's to George Bush's — were broadly and badly overstated.

My remarks describe a bifurcation in the studies of communist Cuba: a native American intelligentsia enthralled with Castro as the shining path of anti-Americanism, and a Cuban exile group who saw in the theory and practice of social science the ultimate and irrefutable rebuke to the tyranny imposed on Cuba after 1959. In some curious way, that same split remains today. Indeed, even the rhetoric harkens to an earlier period. Only a few North Americans have come to appreciate the power of critical social analysis, while scarcely any Cuban exiles have succumbed to the siren calls of anti-American ideology.[16]

The struggle remains the same, running like a dorsal spine through the last thirty-four years of hemispheric relations and world ideologies, and no less from 1933 to 1993 within Cuba. Even if Castro's stay in power has turned out to be more protracted than I, for one, ever imagined, his long denouement has taught us the process of definition. The bifurcations spoken of have come to define the best and the worst in the American and Cuban political landscapes. The process of democratization may be slower than anticipated, even thwarted at times. But the values inherent in that process remain strong and true. In his March 23, 1993, press conference, President Clinton, in defending the *Cuba Democracy Act*, put matters succinctly and in proper causal sequence: first democracy, then elections, followed by policy reconsiderations. Whether the president can adhere to such an ordering of priorities under the constant battering of extremists on both sides remains to be seen.

# NOTES

[1] For an excellent presentation of the theoretical approach herein taken, see Roger B. Mikes, 1991, *Game Theory: Analysis of Conflict* (Cambridge: Harvard University Press) 568 pages. The work is written with particular relevance to social scientific analysis.

[2] Unless otherwise indicated, the references in my article will be drawn from *Consideration of the Cuban Democracy Act of 1992*, 1993, (Washington, D.C.: U.S. Government Printing Office) 563 pages. These hearings before the Committee on Foreign Affairs of the House of Representatives (H.R. 4168 and H.R. 5323) summarize more than the debates; they include relevant data in the formation of the legislation.

[3] Howard W. French, 1993, "The End Has Begun," *The New York Times* (August 8) section 4: 4.

[4] Wayne S. Smith, 1991, "A Pragmatic Cuba Policy," *Foreign Service Journal* (April) 153-157.

[5] Larry Rohter, 1993, "In Miami, Talk of Talking With Cuba," *The New York Times* (June 27) 16.

[6] William Ratliff and Roger Fontaine, 1992, "The End Game," *The Orange County Register* (December 27) 19.

[7] *USA Today*, 1993, "Ease the Trade Embargo on the Cuban People," (June 18) 12A.

[8] Jorge I. Dominguez, 1993, "Secrets of Castro's Staying Power," *Foreign Affairs* 72 (2), 97-107.

[9] Ileana Ros-Lehtinen, 1993, "Keep Pressure on Castro," *USA Today* (June 18) 12A.

[10] John J. Farmer, 1993, "U.S. Need Only Wait for Castro's Cigar to Go Out," *The Star-Ledger* ( June 17) 22.

[11] Linda Robinson, 1993, "Capitalism Comes on Little Cat Feet: The Economy is the Issue in Castro's Cuba," *U.S. News & World Report* (July 28) 42-45.

[12] Donald E. Schulz, 1993, "Can Castro Survive?" *Journal of Interamerican Studies and World Affairs* 35 (1) 113-114.

[13] Larry Rohter, 1993, "Unofficial U.S. Military Group Will Visit Cuba," *The New York Times* (June 29) A9.

[14] Abraham F. Lowenthal, 1993, "Latin America: Ready For Partnership?" *Foreign Affairs* 72 (1) 74-92.

[15] Irving Louis Horowitz, 1993, *The Conscience of Worms and the Cowardice of Lions: Cuban Politics and Culture in an American Context.* Coral Gables: University of Miami, North-South Center; and New Brunswick and London: Transaction Publishers.

[16] See the recent exchange, Jesse Jackson, 1993, "Presiones de la CIA y los ultraderechistas," and Frank Calzon, "La oposición representa el futuro," in *El Nuevo Herald* (December 29) 7A.

# Foreign Investment Opportunities In Cuba: Evaluating the Risks

Antonio Jorge and Robert David Cruz

## Abstract

Between 1989 and 1993, Cuba's economic output declined by as much as 50 percent, and virtually all of the economic gains professed under the revolution have disappeared over this short period. Despite this economic performance and the wave of economic reforms witnessed in many of the former socialist countries and even in China, the Cuban government has failed to acknowledge the need for a fundamental restructuring of Cuba's economic system. Indeed, the economic policy effort has focused on managing the economic crisis rather than on critically examining the island's basic development strategy. The government has not considered fundamental reform of its economy, much less the political system, as a necessary element in its revitalization. The basic pillar of Cuba's economy during the "miracle growth" years of the early 1980s, favorable trade relations with the Soviet bloc, is gone, and the nation has yet to develop an alternative growth model that is viable in today's global economy.

In response to the current economic crisis, Cuba has turned to foreign direct investment (FDI) as the cornerstone of its strategy for lifting the economy out of depression. Although FDI has been permitted in Cuba since 1982, it is only recently that firms have

Antonio Jorge is professor of economics and international relations, Florida International University, Miami. Robert David Cruz is associate professor of economics and international business, Barry University, Miami.

demonstrated an interest in entering into joint ventures in Cuba. While the overwhelming interest has been in tourism and, to a lesser degree, in the extractive industries, the Cuban government hopes to attract investors in nearly all sectors of its economy. This paper examines the risks of FDI in Cuba, highlights the often changing nature of economic policy in Cuba, and questions Cuba's long-term commitment to the policies that it hopes will encourage FDI. The authors note that Cuba has made little progress in demonstrating a long-term commitment to the development of an economic environment that reasonably ensures long-run profitability of investments. Despite the government's efforts to attract foreign investment, considerable uncertainty remains over important issues such as the potential for nationalization, the potential for revisions in the regulations and fiscal incentives that currently make FDI profitable, the long-term stability of the economy, and the long-term stability of the government itself. FDI in different sectors has different degrees of risk, with the lowest risk for those sectors that earn hard currencies and in which profitability is large enough to allow for the recovery of initial capital investment within a relatively short period (two to three years).

## Introduction

As Cuba's economy sank deeper into depression during the early 1990s, the government sought ways to contain the economic crisis without abandoning the fundamental character and objectives of the Cuban Revolution. The government attempted to diversify its export markets, adopted some limited economic reforms, and vigorously sought foreign investors to develop non-traditional export industries. The latter received the highest priority in the government's search for solutions to its most immediate economic problem, the lack of hard currency for imports of energy and intermediate goods. Despite the persistence of an economic depression that began in the late 1980s and the radical changes in the former Soviet Union and East Europe, the Cuban government has yet to acknowledge the need for a major restructuring of its socioeconomic and political system. The failure to recognize the need for fundamental change in economic policy and restructuring of economic and political institutions poses the greatest risk to long-term foreign investment in Cuba.

The government has never viewed social and political reforms as prerequisites for stemming the recent decline in production and income levels nor as necessary elements in the revitalization of the Cuban economy. Recently, Cuba's Foreign Minister, Ricardo Alcaron, proclaimed in an interview given to a Spanish newspaper that his government had no intention of abandoning socialism.[1] In an interview in summer 1993, Carlos Lage, vice president of the Council of State, argued that political reforms were not necessary because Cuba's current problems were economic, not political.[2] This analysis, which asserts a dichotomy between the economy and politics, is an odd view for an official of a Marxist-Leninist government. Nor is this view easy to reconcile with the experience of former socialist countries in Europe and elsewhere. Indeed, the socioeconomic changes that have taken place in the former socialist countries and the economic policy shifts that have taken place in Latin America and the Caribbean provide strong evidence that economic and political problems cannot be easily separated, nor can they be addressed independently of one another. Fidel Castro has declared that there is no aspect of society in which action can be taken without the participation of the Communist Party.[3] Presumably economic policy, therefore, cannot be determined without consideration being given to ideology.

Despite the depressed state of the economy, uncertainty over the long-term viability of the current government, and speculation about potential successors to the current regime, Cuba has attracted some foreign direct investment in the last few years. Since 1989, as many as 108 foreign companies are said to have established joint ventures with the Cuban government,[4] and FDI in Cuba is reported to have reached US$500 million.[5]

Potential investors face questions about the durability of the current investment climate in Cuba. In addition to a microeconomic assessment of each potential investment project, investors must determine whether or not the current economic incentives offered to foreigners represent a long-term shift in Cuba's development strategy. Are the current incentives likely to be retained once the current economic crisis is overcome? The history of post-revolutionary Cuba's economic policy reveals a tendency to change direction abruptly, even when policies appeared to be successful in promoting economic growth.[6] In February 1993, Alcaron, asked about the potential politically destabilizing effect of Cuba's foreign investment initiatives, responded by saying that Cuba had "no other choice but to feed the Trojan horse. We must take a chance. We are familiar with the social and political price, but the real danger is the economic crisis."[7]

The uncertainty over future economic policies and the political stability of the regime represent formidable obstacles to long-term investment in Cuba. To overcome these obstacles the Cuban government has been willing to provide incentives that raise profitability and allow the recovery of capital investment within a short period, and has promised that foreign investors will be free to repatriate profits in the future. Credibility of the regime's commitment to continue the favorable regulatory and fiscal environment is essential to the long-term success of Cuba's foreign investment efforts.

## Economic Policy and Macroeconomic Performance

Cuba's economic policies have undergone significant shifts over the past 34 years.[8] The years immediately after the revolution were characterized by policies of income redistribution and collectivization. During the 1960s Cuba experimented with various socialist models, but by the mid-1970s the government moved to adopt strategies that had been pursued by the Soviets since 1965. Reforms that permitted greater individual economic freedom in the economy and more decentralized economic organization were introduced. In 1986, however, reforms that had been introduced over the previous decade were abruptly reversed, notwithstanding the apparent success of the reforms (the 1980-85 period marked the largest gains in gross output). Nonetheless, the reform policies were characterized as inconsistent with the aims of the revolution, and Castro declared that Cuba's economy had to be *rectified*. The Cuban economy soon returned to a more centralized form of decision making, and, arguably, economic output suffered as a result.

Immediately after the revolution, the government sought to move the economy to a socialist system quickly, attempting to develop its own brand of Marxism while borrowing much from the socialist institutions found in the Soviet Union and Eastern Europe. The Cuban government sought to eliminate material incentives in the workings of the economy and even abolished money in favor of a strict rationing system. During the 1960s the primary focus of economic policy was clearly on the redistribution of wealth and income, and the provision of social services to sectors of society that had been neglected. Economic growth was a secondary priority.

Between 1947 and 1959, US$345 million of foreign direct investment flowed into Cuba. Much of that investment came from U.S. corporations. The government moved swiftly in 1960 to expropriate without compensation $1.8 billion of U.S. assets.[9] Nationalization of domestically owned private property and collectivization of agriculture began shortly thereafter. The government also emphasized consumption and introduced central planning during the early years of the revolution. Economic policy called for diversification of the island's economy, with special emphasis on reducing dependence on sugar exports through a state-directed industrialization program (under Ernesto "Che" Guevara) that proved to be both inefficient and wasteful of scarce capital resources.

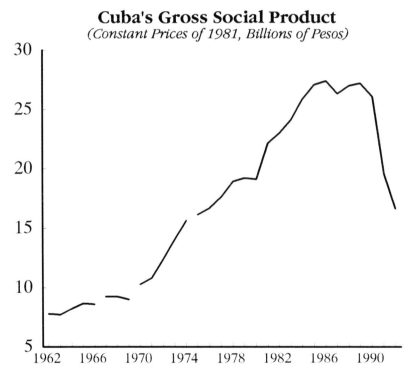

## Cuba's Gross Social Product
*(Constant Prices of 1981, Billions of Pesos)*

Note: GSP at 1981 prices: 1975-1987 are 0official estimates, 88-92 are estimates CIA and A. Zimbalist. 1967-74 based on adjusting official nominal estimates by trend inflation from 1975 to 1987. From 1962-66 nominal GSP + real GSP.

The economy showed only modest growth during the 1960s and, after adjusting for inflation, per capita output probably declined slightly between 1962 and 1969. It is difficult to measure Cuba's macroeconomic performance by Western standards. Cuba's broadest measure of gross output, gross social product (GSP), is not strictly comparable to more standard national accounting measures such as gross domestic product or gross national product.[10] Nonetheless, GSP from 1962 to 1969 grew at an annual rate of 2.1 percent, lagging slightly the rate of population increase.[11] In macroeconomic terms this compared poorly with the performance of the economy during the 1950s (with the exception, of course, of 1958-59). In 1957, Cuba ranked fourth in Latin America in per capita income (behind Venezuela, Argentina and Uruguay) and exceeded the per capita income of Spain and Portugal.[12] However, while the 1960s were a period of significant economic growth for many Latin American countries, Cuba's economy was stagnant.

In 1972 Cuba became a member of the Council for Mutual Economic Assistance (CMEA), entering into special trade relations with the former Soviet Union and other socialist countries. Even before entry into the CMEA, the Soviets had supported the Cuban economy through purchases of Cuban sugar and nickel at prices exceeding world market prices and bartered Soviet petroleum for Cuban sugar, thus permitting Cuban hard currency earnings from resale of Soviet oil on the world market. The official GSP data between 1970 and 1974 show vigorous growth, with GSP increasing some 52 percent (11 percent per year in real terms) over those four years. GSP per capita registered a 41 percent increase over this same period.

The official GSP statistics, however, most likely grossly overstate the amount of growth that actually took place in the early 1970s. The methodology used to calculate GSP during this period, *circulación completa,* is particularly susceptible to double counting as it is based on the summation of the value of goods produced by each enterprise without consideration of the value of inputs required to produce the firm's output.[13] The incidence of double counting thus increases with the number of firms, and during the early 1970s the Cuban government was breaking up large firms into smaller autonomous enterprises. Pérez-López (1991) notes that the number of firms multiplied ten-fold in the early and mid-1970s, and estimates that industrial output grew at a rate of 5.1 percent, significantly lower than official estimates.[14]

In the mid-1970s, Cuba's economic policies witnessed a fundamental change. In 1976, the government introduced the *Sistema de Dirección y Planificación de la Economía* (SDPE), a reform of the existing management and central planning structure. A series of initiatives were adopted between 1976 and 1982 that positively affected the growth of the Cuban economy. With the introduction of SDPE, five basic practices became the guiding principles of economic management. First, profitability in the operation of state enterprises became the performance standard. Second, public enterprises were expected to be self-financing, that is, enterprises were expected (at a minimum) to cover their cost of operation. Third, wage differentials became the primary reward for increased productivity and effort. Fourth, the economic management team acknowledged the use of prices, taxes, and interest rates as basic tools of economic policy, and, fifth, the government seemed to accept a greater decentralization in the micro-level workings of the economy. During this period, farmers' markets were introduced, prices were determined by the interaction of demand and supply, and some self-employed craftsmen (particularly in the construction trades) were allowed to operate.

According to government statistics, the economy responded positively to these incentives. Between 1975 and 1980 GSP grew at an annual adjusted rate of 3.4 percent. As a result, real per capita GSP rose by 14 percent. By 1980 the stimulative effect of these reforms gathered their strongest momentum, and between 1980 and 1985 the economy grew at the unprecedented rate of 7.2 percent per year. Some experts, however, claim that these official estimates are wide of the mark. In any case, by outward measures the SDPE had been quite successful, and a significant transformation of the economy had begun. Between 1980 and 1985, the period of the first five-year plan, the economy was able to achieve a greater degree of diversification. Industry, transportation, and communication each increased as a share of total GSP.

Signs of concern over the emerging transformation in Cuba's economy and economic institutions began to emerge despite the gains in economic growth witnessed over the late 1970s and early 1980s. The central planning agency, JUCEPLAN, had been created to coordinate economic planning functions under the SDPE, but in late 1984 a new administrative group, reporting directly to the Central Committee of the Communist Party, assumed the planning function. Eventually, JUCEPLAN was formally replaced by this new planning group. In February, 1986, Fidel Castro issued a stinging criticism of the SDPE, arguing that it had blindly followed the strategies of the Soviets without considering the unique features of Cuba's socialist society and that it was too preoccupied with profits. Castro remarked that SDPE was leading to the emergence of capitalism within Cuba, and was, therefore, inconsistent with the goals of the revolution. The farmers' markets and self-employment of craftsmen were abolished and economic management recentralized. The most important economic reforms of the previous decade were rescinded, and the nation embarked on the path of *rectification* proclaimed by Castro.

The rectification plan could perhaps not have come at a more adverse time for the Cuban economy. The economic crisis in the Soviet Union and the socialist countries of Eastern Europe placed great strains on the preferential trade relations Cuba enjoyed with those nations. Cuba had been able to overcome much of the effect of the U.S. embargo by highly integrating its economy with those of the former CMEA,[15] particularly with the Soviet economy. Since 1960, the Soviet Union had become both the principal market for Cuba's exports and the principal supplier of imports (oil, in particular). Although Cuba had been able to borrow from non-socialist countries, the Soviet Union was also its major creditor. Cuba had become more dependent on the Soviet Union during the first 30 years of the Cuban Revolution than it had been on the United States in the late 1950s.[16] At the height of the economic expansion of the early 1980s, Cuba sold 55 percent of its exports to the Soviets, and 83 percent of those exports were sugar. By the end of the 1980s Cuba was conducting nearly 85 to 90 percent of its trade with former CMEA countries. As the economies of Cuba's major trading partners contracted, Cuba lost much of its concessionary trade with the former socialist countries, who found themselves in a difficult period of economic transition with severe shortages of hard currency. Both imports and exports suffered.

From 1989 to 1992 Cuba's imports fell from more than $8 billion to approximately $2.25 billion.[17] The low sugar harvest and Cuba's inability to increase non-traditional exports indicate that imports for 1993 may well be below 1992, perhaps falling to between $1.6 and $1.8 billion. The decline in imports of oil from Russia represents the most critical factor in the Cuban economy at present. Oil deliveries fell by more than 50 percent between 1989 and 1992, and they continued to decline over the first half of 1993. Electricity blackouts for as many as 16 hours per day in Havana, and for even longer periods in the countryside, became commonplace. Motor vehicle transportation is at a standstill, and factory production is down significantly due to lack of of spare parts and energy. As much as 70 percent of Cuba's industrial plant is being adversely affected by the current situation.

GSP consequently fell by approximately 40 percent between 1989 and 1992. The level of economic output in 1992 was roughly equivalent, in constant price terms, to the 1976 level. In per capita terms the decline in production represents a return to the 1973 level. Those statistics suggest a decline in living standards that erased all of the gains achieved over 15 years (1973-1988) during just three years (1989-1992). The current depression, however, does not simply represent a return to a standard of living witnessed some two decades ago, because in many ways living conditions are much worse than even in 1959. The seriousness of the current situation may be gauged by the fact that malnutrition and epidemic diseases have become a problem and mortality rates are reportedly climbing. Much of the housing stock is also deteriorating beyond repair. The incidence of theft and other criminal behavior has also been rising sharply, according to press reports. Quantifying the stress on the population is difficult. One indicator, however, is the increased number of people attempting to flee the island in makeshift rafts or hijacked vessels.

## Recent Economic Policy Responses

The government's economic policy response to the crisis has been increased rationing of limited supplies of consumer goods, permitting Cuban citizens to hold dollars and purchase goods in special stores previously reserved for tourists, allowing limited self-employment, and increasing efforts to attract foreign investment, especially in non-traditional export industries (mainly tourism).

The first response to the crisis amounts to virtually a non-policy. That is, the government seeks the economic survival of the country by husbanding its meager resources. Rations have been reduced, labor brigades have been organized, security and repression have increased, rules regarding parallel (or black market) activities go unenforced, and rhetoric is used to boost morale and maintain social unity.

The economic reforms not related to FDI have been extremely limited and designed to alleviate the most immediate problem, the hard currency shortage. In 1993, Cuba expanded the list of consumer goods that exiles could send to relatives on the island, including many foodstuffs (e.g., beans, rice and coffee) that were previously prohibited.[18] Cuba also recently allowed Cuban citizens to hold U.S. dollars (and other hard currencies) and to use hard currency to buy goods in stores previously reserved for tourists, diplomats, and government functionaries. Cuban officials announced this year an increase in the number of visas that it would process for travel from the United States. The objective of these policies is officially to capture some of the dollars that now circulate in the black market and to encourage more exiles to visit the island and spend dollars or to send money to their relatives.

Cuban officials realize that these reforms run the risk of creating sharp economic inequalities among the Cuban population, mainly benefiting those who work in the dollar-earning sectors (principally tourism and related services) and/or those who have generous relatives abroad.[19] The need for foreign exchange, however, is critical, and officials are willing to accept the negative side effects. These reforms have not yet produced any noticeable improvement in the economic situation.

The most significant response to the crisis has been the reforms in Cuba's foreign investment laws and the country's active posture in seeking joint ventures with foreign companies. As early as 1982, Cuba had enacted a joint venture law permitting foreign direct investment. But little FDI activity took place until 1992 when Cuban officials began liberally interpreting the 1982 law. They encouraged foreign investment by offering fiscal incentives such as the exemption of joint ventures from tariff duties on imported materials and from all taxes but social security. Actual terms are negotiated on a case by case basis, with the fiscal incentives often limited to the initial years of the project.[20] Foreign firms were also allowed to conduct business in hard currency, introduce their own management techniques, dismiss workers at their own discretion, set wages, and repatriate profits freely. In July 1992, new legislation permitted the transfer of state property to foreigners, the creation of autonomous (but regulated) enterprises, and the export and import of goods without prior government approval.

The exact number of joint ventures that have resulted from Cuba's efforts is difficult to pin down as various officials and Cuban publications from time to time report different figures. In April 1993, the Cuban office of promotional information reported that 80 joint ventures were currently operating in Cuba.[21] *The Wall Street Journal* in February reported that official statements put the number of joint ventures at

108.[22] Most of the joint ventures (50 percent) have been in tourism, and most of the foreign partners have been from Spain. Of the non-tourist investments, the Cuban government reports 17 Spanish, eight Canadian, six French, and six Mexican companies as joint venture partners. Thus, the number of joint ventures is quite small for an economy of its potential size.

As his rationale for this new economic approach, Castro has suggested that the Chinese model is the ideal remedy for Cuba's economic problems.[23] China's reform and development experience has been markedly different from that of East Europe.[24] Cuba's economic environment is also considerably different from that of China, rendering it unlikely that the successful Chinese reform strategy can be replicated in Cuba.

China began its effort to attract foreign investors in the late 1970s and put in place economic reforms to support the development strategy. At the time, China's economy was largely agricultural, with three-fourths of the labor force employed in agriculture and nearly four-fifths of the population living in rural areas. The initial reforms were aimed at the agricultural sector, thus increasing productivity and releasing resources that could then be directed to the relatively small industrial sector, and especially toward development of local (rural-based) industries. The growth of local industry was in large measure responsible for the high rate of economic growth in China during the past two decades. In the early 1980s, authorities created special economic zones that offered material, fiscal, and labor incentives in strategic geographic locations. Individuals, and not just firms, were afforded greater freedom in economic decision making. The Chinese focused their FDI efforts on manufacturing, with particular emphasis on activities that would introduce new technology into the country. China permitted foreign firms operating in the economic zones to pay higher wages than those in the rest of the country, thus rewarding and stimulating labor productivity increases. Workers resettled in those special areas and often remitted part of their earnings to family members back home or sent home consumer goods purchased within those zones. The economic zones served as small islands of quasi-capitalism within the larger socialist state.

The economic zones were placed in strategic locations where the stimulative effects of reform in the economic incentive system were reinforced by shortages of land and labor in Hong Kong and Taiwan.

Foreign direct investment, originally from expatriate Chinese, linked the growing Chinese manufacturing sector to the expanding market for imports in East and Southeast Asia. China's economy was more closely integrated with the rapidly growing regional economies than with the COMECON group. Thus, when crisis gripped the Soviet Union and the other economies of the Soviet bloc, the Chinese felt little effect; in fact, China was fortunate to execute its economic reforms at a time of rapid growth by its most important trading partners.

The contrasts between China and Cuba are manifest. Cuba's population is already highly urbanized, and the economy is not dominated by agriculture, despite the importance of sugar exports; thus Cuba cannot benefit to the same extent from a shift of resources from agriculture to industry. Cuba has promoted investments in tourism as its highest priority and only recently begun to promote investments in other sectors. Cuba has not yet attempted to link FDI with technology transfer and has moved slowly in allowing greater individual freedom in economic matters. No foreign trade independent of the state is permitted. Despite attempts to increase exports to Europe, Latin America, and Canada, Cuba has been unable to fill the void left by the decline in exports to the former Soviet bloc. These new potential markets have shown little dynamism, and Cuban products have had limited success in market penetration. Cuban industry has been plagued by production bottlenecks largely brought on by the severe contraction in the ability to pay for imports, thus perpetuating a depressionary spiral. Foreign direct investment could, of course, alleviate these constraints, but the key element required to make these investments viable — access to the United States market — remains absent.

Given all these differences, the best that can be said is that while the economic reform process in China may have positive lessons for Cuba, Cuba cannot be said to be following the Chinese model, nor does Cuba enjoy the same external conditions that so aided the development of the Chinese economy.

## Identifying the Risks to Foreign Investors

Cuban authorities have used the rather ambiguous language of the 1982 investment law to negotiate flexible terms with potential investors. But this ambiguity could at some point in the future be detrimental to these investors. Travieso-Diaz (1993) notes that Cuba has not developed a legislative and regulatory framework to protect investors against the potential abuse of the law. The investment law and its implementation rules vest great discretion in the hands of the government, which could act arbitrarily and leave the investor with little recourse against its decisions. The government has established a number of "insurance companies" that provide coverage for unrealized profits due to accidents resulting in production restrictions, import/export insurance protecting against non-payment, and a refinancing insurance that protects against losses to capital. Insurance against political contingencies affecting contract compliance is also available. But these insurance providers are not independent of the government itself, and their willingness and ability to pay out claims (particularly in hard currency) is untested and uncertain.

Further, the foreign investment law does not rule out future nationalizations. The actual language of the law (Article 23, Decree-law 50) guarantees the transfer abroad not only of profits to foreign partners but also proceeds from the sale of a foreign partner's equity interest to a Cuban entity or the foreign partner's share of equity if the association is liquidated.[25] In one publicized case, a Spanish investor was required to relinquish its interest in an entertainment enterprise (with compensation) when Cuban officials decided that its continued operation was not in the best interests of the country. The Cuban government has never relinquished its power to exercise eminent domain against a foreign investor.

Doing business in Cuba may entail significant difficulties as well. Villar reports that his interviews with foreign investors reveal difficulties in cutting through bureaucratic red tape or even understanding the "rules of the game." Villar quotes a Spanish investor's complaints of having to deal with various and sometimes competing ministries. The apparent lack of direction from the top administrators often leaves lower level managers to improvise their own (sometimes inconsistent) regulations and requirements.[26] Mid-level government managers complain that after years of being required to follow strict instructions, they have now been directed to be creative in finding resources and that this has led to personnel tensions. One Canadian entrepreneur with nearly a decade of experience in doing business in Cuba cautions others that doing business there requires a lot more personal attention than doing business in many other parts of the world. Additionally, constrained

0557119

economic resources on occasion prevent Cuban compliance with business agreements, regardless of the government's intentions.[27]

Foreign investors are always subject to the risk of unexpected adverse swings in nominal and real exchange rates, and significant fluctuations in exchange rates are more likely in periods of high inflation. Because Cuba has an administered price system (i.e., prices are set by a government agency) measured inflation has been kept under control, but the large amount of Cuban pesos currently in the hands of residents and the high level of pent-up demand suggest that there exists a considerable amount of "repressed inflation." Cuban officials report an excess supply of cash in local circulation, which has now reached the equivalent of 11 times the monthly wage bill. That is, the typical worker holds cash balances equivalent to 11 months of income. With such a large monetary overhang, the risk of inflation (even hyperinflation) if some prices are allowed to be determined by supply and demand is indeed great.

How might the emergence of significant inflation affect the profitability of foreign investment? The answer to the question depends upon the currency in which revenues are earned and expenses are paid. Most of the joint ventures that have been reported are in the area of tourism or in the production of export goods. In these cases, hard currency is earned by the joint venture, and imported inputs are purchased from those earnings. The remaining proceeds are then used to purchase domestically supplied inputs (e.g., labor) and to allocate the profit to the foreign and Cuban partners. The joint venture must pay its domestic expenses in pesos at a negotiated exchange rate.

In the event of significant inflation, one would expect that production costs paid in local currency would also rise.[28] If no adjustment were made to the exchange rate and the peso were permitted to appreciate in real terms, then the profitability of joint ventures would fall. Similarly, if market reforms that permit state firms to choose between domestic and foreign sources for inputs were introduced, then the demand for imports would rise along with the real appreciation of the currency, further straining foreign exchange reserves and limiting the expansion of domestic industry. In several Latin American countries, appreciation of the real exchange rate has been used in recent years as an anti-inflation strategy. While these policies have been successful in reducing inflation, they have often led to recessionary pressures, severe contractions in industrial activity, and greater income inequality. Will a future Cuban government be willing to accept such costs?

If the currency is devalued, profitability in the export sector may be preserved, but reducing inflation will require even greater reductions in public sector deficits. The latter would likely require increases in taxes and/or fees for public services, reductions in public sector employment, and curtailing public services. Social and political tensions have risen in nearly every country where such policies have been implemented. It is hard to conceive of a scenario in which these measures would be acceptable to the revolutionary government. Indeed, the policy choices that Cuba is likely to confront if it adopts market reforms will be extremely difficult ones.

## Conclusions

The Cuban economy is facing the most serious challenge since the revolution. Cuba has always been a very open economy, highly dependent on exports of basically one crop (sugar) and largely dependent upon one trading partner. Prior to the revolution of 1959, its trade and investment relations with the United States were of paramount importance. Since the revolution, Cuba's economy became more heavily dependent on the Soviet Union than it had been on the United States. Despite early post-revolution attempts to diversify its exports, Cuba has remained highly dependent on sugar exports. This dependence increased because the Soviets transferred significant levels of resources to Cuba by paying higher-than-market prices for Cuban sugar. This distortion had the effect of diverting a greater share of the nation's investment resources to the production of sugar than would have otherwise taken place. This occurred in much the same fashion that a natural resource-rich economy finds it difficult to develop its industrial sector without trade barriers or subsidies.

As the economies of the Soviet Union and Cuba's other socialist trading partners contracted in the late 1980s, Cuba's trade sank and its economy was pushed into its current depression. With the collapse of the Soviet Union and the adoption of market capitalism in most of the former socialist world, the trading environment upon which Cuba's economic development was based collapsed as well. Given the realities of today's world economy, the Cuban economy cannot be revitalized without structural transformation. The economic reforms that Cuba has adopted fall far short of creating that structural transformation.

Cuba's current economic strategy is based on a single policy, the encouragement of foreign direct investment, but the strategy does not address the need to create the  economic institutions required to support FDI and to integrate Cuba in the world economy. Cuba's largest potential market, moreover, remains closed to its products. FDI in Cuba today is fraught with uncertainty and risk, a major reason that FDI has been limited to a few sectors and has gone quite slowly.

# NOTES

[1] "Ricardo Alcaron de Quesada, ministro de asuntos exteriores de Cuba (entrevista)," *País*, February 19, 1993: 10.

[2] Mauricio Cavallo, "Vicepresidente Carlos Lage: Si vas para Cuba— entrevista" (Vice President Carlos Lage: If you go to Cuba—Interview), *El Mercurio* (Santiago de Chile) June 13, 1993. Section D,16.

[3] See Fidel Castro, 1987, "En ninguna parte se puede hacer nada si no está presente el partido," in *Por El Camino Correcto,* Havana: Editora Política.

[4] An April 29, 1993, article in the Russian newspaper *Nezavisimaya Gazeta* quotes a Cuban official as reporting 75 ventures with European and Latin American investors. *The Wall Street Journal* (February 12, 1993) reported 108 joint ventures.

[5] *The Financial Times*, London, July 17-18, 1993, 3.

[6] Fidel Castro surprised observers in 1986 when, in a televised speech, he announced the closure of Cuba's peasant markets on ideological grounds. The 1986 policy shift is discussed further below.

[7] Testimony of Brian Latell, National Intelligence Officer for Latin America, before the U.S. Senate Select Committee on Intelligence, July 29, 1993.

[8] For a brief account of the erratic course of Cuba's economic strategies and policies, see Antonio Jorge, *An Evaluation of Cuba's Post-Revolutionary Socio-Economic Models,* Occasional Paper No. 1984-1, Graduate School of International Studies, University of Miami.

[9] See E.N. Baklanoff, 1975, 112. Approximately 80 percent of U.S. investments were in agriculture (mainly sugar mills), public utilities, and petroleum.

[10] For a discussion of the problem with Cuban statistical measures of the economy, see A. Jorge and J. Salazar (1985) and J. Pérez López (1991). Cuban GSP measures suffer from periodic changes in accounting methodology, which make exact longitudinal comparisons impossible. There exist four unconnected and distinct series of GSP estimates: 1962-1966, 1967-1969, 1970-1974, and 1975-87. The GSP statistic does not fully correct for the problem of double counting for the value of intermediate inputs used in production. In addition, GSP does not include the "value" of services produced. Despite these shortcomings, GSP remains the best available measure of general economic performance for general analysis.

[11] Official statistics for GSP are reported only in nominal terms during this period and, therefore, do not account for price inflation. We have used the trend rate of inflation officially reported over the 1975-1987 period to construct a (trend) deflator. This estimated deflator was then used to convert the nominal series into an estimated real series.

[12] See United Nations, *Yearbook of National Accounts Statistics,* 1962.

[13] See J. Pérez-López, 1991, 12.

[14] Zimbalist and Brundenius (1989) put the estimate of industrial output growth over this period at 7.6 percent per year.

[15] The Council for Mutual Economic Assistance.

[16] J. Pérez-López, 1991, 26.

[17] *The Washington Times,* January 3, 1993, 8A.

[18] The shipping charges, as high as US$40 per pound, inhibit more goods from arriving in Cuba.

[19] This policy may even aid those who engage in criminal activity from petty theft to narcotics trafficking and prostitution.

[20] *Business Tips on Cuba,* 1993, (March) 2.

[21] See *Business Tips on Cuba,* 1993, (April) 4.

[22] "The Trials and Tribulations of Cuba's Managers," *The Wall Street Journal,* February 12, 1993, A15.

[23] "Glavnoye vystoyat. No kak?" (The most important thing is to survive. But how?), *Za rubezhom* (Moscow), March 12-18, 1993, 11-12.

[24] F.G. Adams, 1993, discusses the economic transition in China in "Economic Transition in China and Eastern Europe: Are There Lessons to be Learned?" University of Pennsylvania, mimeo (December).

[25] *Business Tips on Cuba,* 1993, (March) 2.

[26] See A. Villar, "The Trials and Tribulations of Cuba's Managers," *The Wall Street Journal,* February 12, 1993, A15.

[27] See interview with John Emery, "Cuba Libre?" *Globe and Mail,* September 1992, 23-25.

[28] Otherwise, the real value of payments made to domestic labor and domestic inputs would fall, and the distribution of income would shift in favor of the joint ventures. One would expect that a significant distributional shift in favor of joint ventures would not be permitted to continue unchecked.

## SELECTED BIBLIOGRAPHY

Adams, F.G. 1993. "Economic Transition in China and Eastern Europe: Are There Lessons to be Learned?" University of Pennsylvania, mimeo.

Baklanoff, Eric N. 1975. *Expropriation of U.S. Investments in Cuba, Mexico and Chile.* New York: Praeger Publishers.

*Business Tips on Cuba.* March 1993.

*Business Tips on Cuba.* April 1993.

Jorge, Antonio. 1984. *An Evaluation of Cuba's Post-Revolutionary Socio-economic Models.* Occasional Paper No. 1984-1. Coral Gables: Graduate School of International Studies, University of Miami.

Jorge, Antonio. 1985. "Growth with Equity: The Failure of the Cuban Case." *Inter-American Review of Bibliography* 35, 1: 48-62. Washington, D.C.: Organization of American States.

Jorge, Antonio. 1989. "Ideology, Planning, Efficiency and Growth: Change Without Development." In *Cuban Communism*, ed. Irving Horowitz. New Brunswick: Transaction Publishers.

Jorge, Antonio, and Jorge Salazar-Carrillo. 1985. "The Price System in a Socialist Economy: The Cuban Case." *The Southeastern Latin-Americanist* 29, 1: 1-8.

Pérez-López, Jorge. 1991. "Bringing the Cuban Economy into Focus." *The Latin American Research Review* 26, 3: 7-53.

Ross, Oakland. 1992. "Cuba Libre?" *Globe and Mail, Report on Business.* (September).

Rúa del Llano, Manuel, and Pedro Monreal. 1993a. "Cuba: Promotion of Foreign Investment." *Business Tips on Cuba* 1, 7: 1-2.

Rúa del Llano, Manuel, and Pedro Monreal. 1993b. "Cuba's Open-Door Economic Policy." *Business Tips on Cuba* 1, 6: 2.

Travieso-Diaz, Matias. 1993. "Is Cuba Stealing Pages from China's Development Program?" *The Wall Street Journal,* January 8, A15.

United Nations. 1962. *Yearbook of National Accounts Statistics.* New York: United Nations.

Villar, Arturo. 1993. "The Trials and Tribulations of Cuba's Managers." *The Wall Street Journal*, February 12, A15.

Zimbalist, A., and C. Brundenius. 1989. *The Cuban Economy: Measurement and Analysis of Socialist Performance*. Baltimore: Johns Hopkins University Press.

# CREDITORS' RIGHTS: CLAIMS AGAINST CUBAN CONFISCATED ASSETS

## Robert C. Helander

## Introduction

P otential investors in Cuba are faced with uncertainty until the status of claims for expropriation are resolved. If compensation or restitution is not agreed, investors may find those investments clouded by uncertain rights and unclear titles.

The United States passed the Cuban Claims Act in 1964, granting authority to the Foreign Claims Settlement Commission to adjudicate the validity and amount (over US $1.8 billion) of claims by U.S. citizens whose property was taken by the Castro government. But no money was appropriated to pay those claims, and the total, with over thirty years of interest added, has grown. Claims for property taken from non-U.S. citizens at the time are estimated to be several times greater.

The resolution of these claims will affect negotiations leading to the end of the Castro regime and the establishment of a democratic Cuba.

Cuba is currently tempting foreign investment in a variety of businesses ranging from tourism to manufacturing. When the assets employed in those activities include land, buildings, or businesses that were expropriated but not compensated by the Castro government,

Robert C. Helander, Esq. practices international corporate law with the firm of Kaye, Scholer, Fierman, Hays & Handler, New York, and has advised Latin American governments and private companies on privatization and financing ventures. He is a member of the Council of the Americas, the Council on Foreign Relations, the Pan American Society, the Americas Fund for Independent Universities, and many other international organizations.

potential foreign investors need to ask themselves what risks they run.[1]

The answer may not be easy to come by in the case of assets taken from U.S. citizens. To assess the risk, it is necessary to understand the legal framework that has preserved these claims for more than thirty years.

The United States has a history of verifying and quantifying claims of U.S. individuals and of corporations in which the majority interest is owned by U.S. individuals. Prior to World War II, there had developed an international law of state responsibility toward aliens, derived from a series of cases in which individual claims were pursued before international tribunals. But World War II and the waves of economic nationalism that accompanied the birth of new nations created so many claims that the United States, and other developed countries, adopted lump sum procedures whereby the claims of their nationals were negotiated ("espoused" in diplomatic terminology) with the "taking state," which would agree to pay a lump sum payment in exchange for the extinguishment of all claims. The espousing state would then use the assets (which might include frozen accounts, fresh cash, installment payments, and payment in kind of raw materials or other assets) received from the "taking state" and pay its nationals' claims, much as a trustee in bankruptcy distributes fractional shares of assets to creditors. Those payments never seemed to rise to the value of what was taken by the offending state.

In 1949, Congress passed the International Claims Settlement Act, thus creating the International Claims Commission. There already existed a War Claims Commission that administered claims under the War Claims Act of 1948. In 1954, Congress transferred the functions and authorities of both bodies to the Foreign Claims Settlement Commission of the United States (FCSC).[2]

The FCSC has administered some forty programs in countries ranging from Poland to Ethiopia in which over 660,000 claims have been processed and over US$3 billion in awards certified. That works out to less than US$5,000 per claim, but that statistic is as misleading as saying that the average height of professional jockeys and basketball players is five feet, nine inches.

In 1964, Congress added Title V (the "Cuban Claims Act")[3] to the International Claims Settlement Act, specifically to deal with claims by U.S. nationals against Cuba. At the time, claims were estimated to total more than US$1 billion. Congress had initially thought the claims could be settled out of frozen Cuban assets, but the U.S. Treasury Department estimated that only US$50 million to US$60 million were available, and Congress was unwilling to appropriate money from general revenue to fund a recovery pool. Thus Title V did not actually provide for payment; rather, it established a mechanism for the adjudication and quantification of claims before evidence and witnesses as to the events of 1959-1961 were no longer available.

By 1972 when the FCSC submitted its Final Report of the Cuban Claims Program to the Congress, it had dealt with 8,816 claims, totalling US$3.3 billion.[4] One-third of the claims were rejected, and a total of US$1.8 billion was certified as owing, an average of US$304,000 per claim.[5] The FCSC stated:

> Although ... the Act did not expressly provide for the inclusion of interest on the amount allowed, the Commission concluded that interest should be added in a certifiable loss in conformity with principles of international law, justice and equity, and should be computed from the date of loss to the date of any future settlement. (See the *Claim of American Cast Iron Pipe Company*, Claim No. CU-0249, 25 FCSC Semiann. Rep. 49 (July-Dec. 1966).[6]

One can debate the present value of the certified claims with interest after thirty years, but the amount is clearly large. Will it loom large in discussions of an eventual return of Cuba to the family of nations?

The Cuban claims are peculiar in many respects. By contrast, when the United States in 1974 negotiated the settlement of the claims arising out of the progressive takings in Peru after the 1968 coup d'état, those claims were only a few years old, and there were a limited number of claimants, mainly corporations whose interest in and prospects for further business in Peru were doubtful at best. No one was happy with the settlement amounts, but all claimants were willing to close the dispute, take their shares of the US$76 million settlement, and turn to other business.[7]

Even the tax laws of the United States have been affected by the Cuban experience. Normally, losses to personal property caused by confiscation by a foreign country are not considered, for tax purposes, to be casualty or theft losses. However, in 1964 the rule was amended[8] in the specific case of Cuba to qualify the fair market value of such losses as deductible if the losses were sustained by an individual who was a U.S. citizen or resident alien on December 31, 1958. The tax laws were changed again in 1971 to permit the deduction of losses of investment property against ordinary income without limitation.[9]

Cuba is a special case for the United States. After Fidel Castro came to power, the cream of Cuba's intellectual and entrepreneurial population (who could) voted with their feet, and most came only "ninety miles away." They have followed events in Cuba with the same energy and intelligence that they have applied to creating a resoundingly successful new life in the United States. It should come as no surprise that people who once spurned political involvement in Havana have become expert participants in the politics of the United States and have a special interest in how the end game with the Castro regime should be played.

The Cuban Democracy Act of 1992[10] is but one expression of the impact of Cuban-Americans on the issue. Under that law, no concession to the current regime seems likely. Clearly, a settlement of outstanding U.S. claims will be complicated. The proponents of a hard line toward Cuba might be expected to support a tough line on settlement numbers.

On the other hand, most of the so-called "Cuban lobby" are not qualified claimants under the Cuban Claims Act, which required that claimants be individual U.S. citizens or corporations 50 percent of the shares of which were owned by U.S. citizens at the time of the taking and who continued to own the claim until the time of the filing with the FCSC. So, other than a few individuals or their heirs, the claimants will mostly be corporations who have long since written off their claims. This being the case, why should the outstanding claims get the attention of non-claimants? One reason is that they may provide indirect political leverage. U.S. citizens who own these claims are, absent legislation by Congress, foreclosed from pursuing any remedies against the Government of Cuba outside the lump sum negotiations. The law is settled that a participant in a lump sum quantification program is bound by whatever result is reached in negotiations at the governmental level and has no other recourse or appeal.[11] But claimants may make common cause with those who resist any weakening of the U.S. position on Cuba in order to extract a settlement closer to the certified amounts and add interest from the date of the taking.

The alliance between those who oppose any soft line on settlement of outstanding disputes with the Castro regime and U.S. claimants could fall apart at any moment. Should the government of Cuba change and new leadership more acceptable to the United States take over, one could imagine that there would be tremendous pressure from the present opponents of Castro to authorize aid programs for reconstruction for a new Cuba. The political situation in the United States would quickly reverse, and the outstanding claims could represent a serious obstacle to quick passage of an aid bill. In 1963, Congress passed the Hickenlooper Amendment to the Foreign Assistance Act of 1961, authorizing the president to suspend assistance to any government that has taken U.S. property without complying with the obligation under international law to make prompt, effective, and fair compensation. The threat of Hickenlooper hangs over every taking where the United States has a potential interest in moving toward closer ties in the immediate future. The State Department, to which the president usually delegates the negotiation of lump sum agreements, may find itself trying to balance foreign policy goals with the pressures of claimants who want amounts as close to one hundred cents on the dollar as they can get in settlement.

Timing and the intricacies of Cuban and domestic U.S. politics will have a significant impact on negotiations for the settlement of U.S. claims. But the Cuba Claims Act does not affect claims by anyone who was not a U.S. citizen from the time a claim arose until it was filed with the FCSC. What about Cubans and other nationals who have subsequently become U.S. citizens? Since they will not be bound by any lump sum agreement, can they bring their individual claims in U.S. courts?

There is little chance that a U.S. court would adjudicate such claims, in part because of the act of state doctrine, which holds that U.S. courts will not sit in judgment on the actions of a foreign sovereign state. The Hickenlooper Amendment seeks to remedy this by other means, but it only addresses claims from those who were U.S. citizens at the time of the taking. But, would it seem fair for people who have been U.S. citizens for almost three decades to be denied some means of seeking compensation for losses they or their parents sustained prior to becoming U.S. citizens? It is predictable that someone will suggest an amendment to the Cuban Claims Act to permit these claims to go forward.

Passage of such legislation would pose additional uncertainties for anyone contemplating the purchase of Cuban assets. If Congress were to open the U.S. courts, or the FCSC, to such claims and provide funding, U.S. citizens now bound by the original Cuban Claims Act and the determination of the FCSC would clamor for equal treatment. Given the current emphasis on deficit reduction, it is unlikely that such legislation would include funding by the Congress. But, without funding, a new set of claims would cast further doubts over any negotiations with a newly democratic Cuba. Absent an agreement by a new government of Cuba and the United States to establish a tribunal, perhaps along the lines of the Iran-United States Arbitral Tribunal in The Hague, these claimants may be without a remedy or a forum in which to pursue a remedy.

There is a further complication to the way the claims procedure may play out — restitution. Given the magnitude of the emigration from Cuba to the United States, the size of the claims, covered and not covered under the Cuba Claims Act, and the bankruptcy of Cuba, one could imagine that there will be pressure for restitution, if monetary damages are not feasible.

Restitution could be attractive to a democratic but impoverished Cuba. Restitution could be a complement or even a substitute for privatization in many cases, bringing entrepreneurial skills back to assets which have foundered during three decades of Leninist economics. Short of a massive infusion of aid from the United States, the choice for claimants under both the existing legislation and any newly authorized categories may be between pennies on the dollar in a lump sum arrangement or another chance to utilize their former assets. If a post-Castro Cuba were to offer restitution in selected cases, one could imagine a brisk secondary market developing for the purchase of those opportunities.

Non-U.S. investors who are tempted to move into Cuba before the claims settlement negotiations are concluded might be wise to buy the rights of former owners to avoid problems in the future. There is enough uncertainty in any business without having to worry about claims against the legal title to physical assets central to the operation. Arguably, the price of peace of mind will only increase as the day of Cuban liberation draws nearer.

The resolution of the long-standing problem of Cuban claims may have as much to do with the art of political negotiation as it will with legal advocacy and international law.

**Figure 1.**

Final Statistical Report on Cuban Claims Program

| Type | Number Filed | $ Amount Claimed | Number Denied* | $ Amount Denied | Number Awarded | $ Amount Awarded |
|------|-------|-------|-------|-------|-------|-------|
| Corporate | 1,146 | 2,855,993,212.69 | 248 | 1,277,494,373.14 | 898 | 1,578,498,839.55 |
| Individual | 7,670 | 490,413,058.67 | 947 | 269,363,329.53 | 5,013 | 221,049,729.14 |
| Totals | 8,816 | 3,346,406,271.36 | 1,195 | 1,546,857,702.67 | 5,911 | 1,799,548,568.69 |

* Additional claims totaling 1,710 were dismissed without consideration by the commission or withdrawn by claimants.

Source: *Foreign Claims Settlement Commission 1972 Annual Report,* Washington, D.C., 412.

**Figure 2.**

Analysis of Final Awards Granted under the Cuban Claims Program
As of July 6, 1972

| Amount of Awards | To Corporations | To Individuals | Total |
|------|-------|-------|-------|
| $1,000 or less ....................... | 63 | 1252 | 1315 |
| 1,001 to 5,000 ..................... | 195 | 1701 | 1896 |
| 5,001 to 10,000 ................... | 100 | 640 | 740 |
| 10,001 to 25,000 ................. | 134 | 593 | 727 |
| 25,001 to 50,000 ................. | 89 | 328 | 417 |
| 50,001 to 100,000................ | 51 | 208 | 259 |
| 100,001 to 250,000.............. | 77 | 145 | 222 |
| 250,001 to 500,000.............. | 56 | 74 | 130 |
| 500,001 to 1,000,000 ........... | 41 | 33 | 74 |
| Over $1,000,000................... | 92 | 39 | 131 |
| TOTAL ................................ | 898 | 5013 | 5911 |

Source: *Foreign Claims Settlement Commission 1972 Annual Report,* Washington, D.C., 413.

**Figure 3.**

Ten Highest Certifications of Loss under the Cuban Claims Program

| Claim No. | Dec. No. | Claimant | Amount of Award | |
|---|---|---|---|---|
| CU-2578 | CU-4122 | Cuban Electric Company | | $267,568,413.62 |
| CU-2615 | CU-5013 | International Telephone & Telegraph Corporation | $50,676,963.88 | |
| | | International Telephone & Telegraph Corporation as Trustee | $80,002,794.14 | 130,679,758.02 |
| CU-2622 | CU-3578 | North American Sugar Industries, Inc. | $97,373,414.72 | |
| | | Cuban-American Mercantile Corp. | $52,688.46 | |
| | | West India Company | $11,548,959.95 | 108,975,063.13 |
| CU-2619 | CU-6049 | Moa Bay Mining Company | | 88,349,000.00 |
| CU-2573 | | Cuban American Nickel Co. | | Denied |
| CU-2776 | CU-3824 | United Fruit Sugar Company | | 85,110,147.09 |
| CU-0665 | CU-5060 | West Indies Sugar Company | | 84,880,957.55 |
| CU-2445 | CU-3969 | American Sugar Company | | 81,011,240.24 |
| CU-0938 | CU-3838 | Standard Oil Company | | 71,611,002.90 |
| CU-2156 | CU-6034 | Bangor Punta Corporation | $39,078,904.64 | |
| | | Baraqua Industrial Corp. | 6,280,722.17 | |
| | | Florida Industrial Corporation of New York | 3,749.751.18 | |
| | | Macareno Industrial Corporation of New York | 4,145,316.01 | |
| | | Bangor Punta Operations | 124,429.06 | 53,379,123.06 |
| CU-1331 | CU-4546 | Texaco Inc. | | 50,081.109.67 |

Source: *Foreign Claims Settlement Commission 1972 Annual Report*, Washington, D.C., 414.

# *Appendix I.*

### PERU

Settlement of Certain Claims

Agreement signed at Lima February 19, 1974;
Entered into force February 19, 1974.

## Agreement Between the Government of The United States of America and The Government of Peru

The Government of the United States of America and the Government of Peru issued the following statement on August 9, 1973:

"At the initiative of the Government of the United States of America, the Revolutionary Government of the Armed Forces of Peru has agreed to hold conversations with the objective of considering certain aspects of some United States investments. For this purpose, President Nixon has designated Mr. James R. Greene as his special emissary.

"It has been clearly established by the Government of Peru that the IPC case will not for any reason be a subject of said conversations inasmuch as this is a matter which has been definitively resolved. The Government of the United States recognizes that this is the position of the Revolutionary Government.

"The conversations will observe the most complete respect for the autonomous and sovereign decisions of both governments as well as for the profound transformation being carried out by the Revolutionary Government of the Armed Force of Peru.

"The two governments agree that the conversations will contribute to the improvement of their relations, making them more cordial and constructive."

As a result of those conversations, the Government of the United States and the Government of Peru, desirous of arriving at a solution of pending problems, and with the objective of definitively concluding them and avoiding the presentation of future claims on these matters, have decided to conclude the following Agreement:

## Article I

A. The pending problems to which this Agreement refers are the claims of United States nationals arising prior to the date of this Agreement as a result of expropriation or other forms of permanent taking by the Revolutionary Government of the Armed Forces of Peru of property and interests in property, direct or indirect, and the claims of the Government of Peru against such United States nationals, as well as the claims of United States nationals and the Government of Peru over certain road construction contracts arising prior to the date of this Agreement.

B. "United States nationals" as used in this Agreement means corporations organized under the laws of a state of the United States which (a) own individually or collectively, directly or indirectly, 50 percent or more of the outstanding stock or other property or interest in property or contract rights, upon which the claims referred to in paragraph A are based, and (b) have made their claims known to the United States Government prior to the date of this Agreement.

C. The provisions of this Agreement shall not affect in any way any claims of citizens or corporations of the United States or Peru against the other government which, because of the provisions of this article, do not come within the scope of this Agreement.

## Article II

A. In order to resolve these pending problems and as a total and definitive solution, a settlement is agreed upon, after taking into account the claims of the Government of Peru against the aforesaid United States nationals or their subsidiaries, branches or affiliates in Peru, in the amount of $76,000,000 which sum will be delivered to the Government of the United States in settlement for the properties, interests, or rights forming the subject of the Agreement, and in discharge of any liability or obligation of the Government of Peru with respect to the claims of the United States nationals referred to in Article I.

B. The aforesaid amount, $76,000,000, will be delivered by the Government of Peru to the Government of the United States upon signature of this Agreement, thus resolving any claims of nationals of the United States against the Government of Peru regarding the matters covered by this Agreement.

## Article III

The distribution of the sum referred to in Article II hereof falls within the exclusive competence of the Government of the United States, without any responsibility arising therefrom on the part of the Government of Peru from the exercise of this authority by the Government of the United States. In accordance with internal procedures falling within its exclusive competence, the Government of the United States will deposit said sum in a trust account in the United States Treasury until distribution, with interest, pursuant to the determination by the Secretary of State of the United States of America in accordance with the laws of the United States.

## Article IV

The Government of the United States declares that the payment of the sum referred to in Article II cancels any liability or obligation of the Government of Peru to United States nationals, their subsidiaries, branches and affiliates,in respect of the problems and claims referred to in Article I.

## Article V

In view of the intergovernmental nature of this Agreement, the Government of Peru declares that there no longer exist any liabilities for the payment of taxes, other charges, or obligations, or legal actions, civil or otherwise, against the United States nationals referred to in Article I, their subsidiaries, branches or affiliates in Peru, or against the present or former officials of any of them, regarding their activities as employees of said nationals, their subsidiaries, branches or affiliates prior to the signing of this Agreement, nor will any claims or proceeding based upon such taxes, charges, obligations, liabilities, or legal actions affecting the natural or juridical persons referred to above be asserted, continued, or enforced in the future. The Government of Peru will also assume the legally valid contractual and other pecuniary obligations (including pensions and other employee benefits) of the United States nationals, their subsidiaries, branches or affiliates in Peru referred to in Article I, which arise out of their operations in Peru and are communicated to the Government of Peru.

## Article VI

The Government of the United States will undertake to obtain, where pertinent, from the United States nationals referred to in Article I the documents or titles related to their claims or to the satisfaction thereof and deliver them to the Government of Peru.

## Article VII

After the entry into force of this Agreement, neither government will present to the other, on its behalf or on behalf of another, any claim or demand with respect to the matters referred to in Article I of this Agreement. In the event that such claims are presented directly by nationals of one country to the government of the other, such government will refer them to the government of the national concerned.

## Article VIII

This Agreement shall enter into force upon signature and upon payment in accordance with Article II. (See Annexes A and B.)

Done at Lima this 19th day of February, 1974, in duplicate in the Spanish and English languages, both texts being equally authentic.

For The Government of the United States of America:

James R. Greene      Taylor G. Belcher

For The Government of Peru:

Miguel A. de la Flor Valle

## Annex A

Without modifying the provisions of this Agreement, the Government of Peru expressly states that the matters covered by this Agreement refer to the problems and claims arising from the activities carried on in Peru by the following companies:

Peruvian Branch of Cerro de Pasco Corporation incorporated in the State of Delaware

United States Sociedad Paramonga Limitada S.A.

Compañia Papelera Trujillo S.A. (TRUPAL)

Cartavio S.A.

Envases Sanmarti S.A.

Cargill Peruana S.A.

Gloucester Peruvian S.A.

Pesquera Meilan S.A.

Gold Kist S.A. and Pesquera Salinas S.A.

Compañia Pesquera de Coishco S.A.

Refineria Conchan-Chevron S.A. and Compañia Petrolera Conchan-Chevron S.A.

Brown and Root Overseas Inc. and Brown and Root S.A.

Morrison Knudsen Company Inc. (EMKAY) and its associates

Conselva Zachry International Inc. and its associates

## Annex B

The Government of the United States recognizes that the position of the Government of Peru is stated in Annex A and notes that this position is stated without modifying, by interpretation or otherwise, the provisions of this Agreement.

# NOTES

[1] See "Trading with the U.S. Enemy — Mexican Trade and Investment with Cuba Are Taking Off," *El Financiero Weekly International Edition* (April 12, 1993) 1, 14-15.

[2] International Claims Settlement Act of 1949, as amended, 22 U.S.C. 1621-1627.

[3] International Claims Settlement Act of 1949, as amended, 22 U.S.C. 1624-1642.

[4] The value of non-qualifying claims by Cuban exiles has been estimated to exceed US$7.1 billion in 1958 dollars. See José F. Alonso and Armando M. Lago, 1993, "A First Approximation of the Foreign Assistance Requirements of a Democratic Cuba," preliminary research data, unpublished paper.

[5] Statistical tables attached to this chapter are reproduced as Figures 1 and 2.

[6] *Final Report of the Cuban Claims Program* reprinted from the *Foreign Claims Settlement Commission 1972 Annual Report* (to U.S. Congress), 76.

[7] The English text of the *Agreement Between the Government of the United States of America and the Government of Peru* is reproduced as Appendix I of this chapter.

[8] Internal Revenue Code (IRC), Section 165(i), 26 U.S.C. 165 (i), was added by the Revenue Act of 1964, Pub. L. No. 88-272, approved February 26, 1964.

[9] Internal Revenue Code (IRC) Section 165 (i), 26 U.S.C. 165 (i), was amended by Pub. L. No. 91-677 ("An Act to Amend Provisions of the Internal Revenue Code of 1954 Relating to the Treatment of Certain Losses Sustained by Reason of the Confiscation of Property by the Government of Cuba"), approved January 12, 1971.

[10] Cuban Democracy Act of 1992, 22 U.S.C. 6001-6010.

[11] "Once it has espoused a claim, [the Executive] has wide-ranging discretion in disposing of it. It may compromise it, seek to enforce it, or waive it entirely." Asociación de Reclamantes v. United Mexican States, 735 F.2d 1517, 1523 (D.C. Cir. 1984).

# Investing in Cuba: A Personal View

Otto J. Reich

It is a pleasure to be back in Canada. Canadians always say that Americans don't know as much about Canada as Canadians do about the United States. I think that's changing. When I told a friend that I was coming here, he volunteered that he is a big fan of your President, Tim Campbell. He can't fool me. I know your president's name is Kim, not Tim.

Obviously, I'm kidding about [former] Prime Minister Campbell, but it is true that Canadians tend to follow U.S. politics more closely than we Americans do yours. I wonder, however, how many of you remember the name of Ross Perot's vice-presidential running-mate in the last elections? Although he was a war hero, he was not very well-known in the states either, until the vice-presidential debate, when he asked what were probably the two most profound questions of the campaign. When his turn came to speak to a nationwide audience, Admiral James Stockdale turned to the camera and said: "Who am I, and what am I doing here?"

I have been asked to speak about the problems and prospects of investing in Cuba, and I will. But first I, too, want to answer Admiral Stockdale's questions. I don't even know the Admiral, nor did I vote

---

Otto J. Reich is a partner in the Brock Group, a Washington international trade consulting firm. He has held several positions in the U.S. government, including U.S. ambassador to Venezuela, special advisor to the secretary of state, and assistant administrator of the U.S. Agency for International Development. He has lived and worked in several Latin American countries and has degrees from Georgetown University and the University of North Carolina at Chapel Hill. He is a native of Cuba.

for his ticket, but I do think his questions are relevant. Why should you be interested in my opinion about investing in Cuba?

I was born in Cuba. My father was an Austrian Jew and my mother a Cuban Catholic. In August 1938, six months after the Nazi annexation of Austria, after numerous beatings by Nazi thugs, my father, in justified fear for his life, left Vienna and traveled 700 kilometers by motorcycle with his childhood friend, a Catholic.

At the Swiss border they said goodbye, and my father climbed through the Alps, where he had hiked a boy, until he reached Switzerland. He telegraphed a prearranged message to his parents to let them know he was safe. He walked and hitchhiked his way to France where he would find work and begin to try to find a way to get his parents out of Austria. In September 1939, the war broke out. As a foreigner, he joined the French Foreign Legion, as did thousands of other Central European refugees, to fight the Nazis who had invaded his homeland. He was trained as a legionnaire and sent to North Africa. As we all know, when the Germans invaded France, the fighting did not last long, and the French capitulated. The Vichy regime theoretically guaranteed the safety of all legionnaires who had fled Nazi-occupied Europe. He made his way to Casablanca, Serpa Pinto, and Havana. From Cuba he came to the United States.

Why is this background relevant to this discussion? Why does it matter that my family history, like so many others in both our countries, is fraught with totalitarian nightmares? I have studied what happened in Europe in the thirties and forties and what has happened in Cuba since the sixties, not just because it happened to my family, but because there are parallels.

Then, as now, people rationalized doing business with dictatorships saying, "If we don't, someone else will;" or "This is the way to bring them around, make them part of the civilized world; by dealing with them we moderate their behavior. By not dealing with them, we simply isolate them and strengthen the hard-liners among them."

Or put another way, why should morality stand in the way of a good business deal? Actually, that may be too cynical a way of looking at it. Very few business people are so cruel that they would purposely assist a dictator who is torturing, killing, and starving people — just so they can make a few bucks. So rationalization becomes necessary.

There is a natural desire to feel that dealing with any country is good. Thus, those business people point to the good they are doing, to their contributions to economic development and job creation. Or they convince themselves of the popularity of the leaders and say that it is the critics that are wrong.

When are we going to learn? Are the lessons of having tried to "modify the behavior" of the Japanese in the days leading up to December 1941 not enough? The scrap iron the United States had sold to Japan was returned at Pearl Harbor in the form of bombs. Are the lessons of having dealt with Hitler, as Sweden did until 1943, or as Argentina did, until 1944, not enough?

As far as helping economic development, let us not forget that Hitler built the autobahns, Mussolini made the trains run on time, and Stalin industrialized Russia. And they all were quite successful at acquiring real estate, to boot! In fact, few leaders have been as successful at job creation as the totalitarians. And, in case someone wonders about their popularity, real or apparent, just take a look at the Movietone newsreels of the rallies in Berlin, Rome, and Moscow.

The subject of this seminar is problems and prospects of investing in Cuba. From the excellent panelists who have gathered here, you will hear that there may indeed be opportunities for investment in Cuba today. You will also hear that there are also many practical problems associated with doing business in Cuba.

The types of problems associated with investing in Cuba are varied: political, economic, commercial, legal, ethical, and moral. It is my opinion that when taken together, these problems far outweigh any short-term benefits of investing in Cuba.

I hope you will also hear that there may be better opportunities for doing real business with a post-Castro, democratic, free-market Cuba than with the current communist government of the island. And I want to add that this may be an "either/or" situation — either wait for a change, or deal with one of the last remaining bastions of Leninist ideology left in the world.

It is my opinion that the foreign companies doing business with the Castro government today are not only taking a very large risk because of the lack of juridical and other protections normally afforded business persons in a free society, but also risking their investments because of the probability of political upheavals that will turn the current policies of the Castro government upside down.

Cubans inside and outside the island have been predicting the end of the Castro dictatorship for decades. These groups often disagree about just about everything. But in a rare show of unity that should serve as a warning to any prudent investor, last year a group of eleven Cuban exile organizations based in several nations issued an "Open Letter to Investors," in which they stated the following:

"Commercially, it is not wise to invest in an island ruled by a one-party state, with no recourse to any non-governmental institutions because none exist. Recently, a Spanish group, judging that the risks were not so severe, began to invest in Cuba. Suddenly the group was forced to stop a hotel investment in the Isle of Pines because the government of Cuba failed to meet its obligations to the project."

The Gruexva consortium was forced to stop building a complex of over three thousand hotel rooms, costing over $200 million, because the government of Cuba had reneged on its commitment to build the necessary infrastructure — roads, water supply, electrical energy — required by the project. Earlier last year, Havana Club Discotheque, which had been highlighted as a successful example of a joint venture between the Cuban government and a Spanish firm, was suddenly nationalized by Fidel Castro.

What makes these sudden cancellations all the more noteworthy is that they fall in the sector with the highest priority for the Castro government — tourism. It is not a secret that Castro hopes that the quick infusion of foreign exchange provided by tourism will give his government the necessary oxygen to breathe some life into a moribund body politic.

From an economic standpoint, it makes no sense to invest in an island whose gross domestic product (GDP) has dropped by 50 percent in four years. So desperate is the Cuban government for foreign exchange that it is selling compensation in clear violation of Cuban and international law. I am sure lawyers will be making considerable fortunes after the fall of Castro, trying to determine the legality of the actions of his government in the past thirty-five years. The political solution, however, may not be so difficult to decipher. It is difficult to envision a post-Castro Cuba in which those persons who collaborated with a thirty-five year dictatorship will be allowed to keep the fruits of their investments without some very high costs.

From a political standpoint, it makes no sense to invest in an island where the government relies on force to stay in power and where it appears that the end is near. In the past few months there have been increasing numbers of reports coming out of Cuba of violence against the visible presence of the government and, more ominously for the subject of this conference, for the foreign investment which supports it.

While the people of Cuba are and will probably continue to be friendly toward individual visitors to the island, there are press reports of rocks, bricks, and other missiles being hurled at government buildings, diplomatic or hard-currency stores, and, more recently, the homes of Communist party officials.

On August 28, 1993, in the town of San Miguel del Padron, province of Havana, the Cuban police entered a home to arrest a fugitive. They dragged the man, whom they had beaten and bloodied and tied hand and foot, into the street (the man's name is Julio Rancol Santana). They continued beating the man as they threw him unconscious into the police car. The crowd that had gathered then turned on the policemen, beating them severely. One of the policemen managed to call for help. Fifteen patrol cars converged on the scene, which by then had attracted what is described by eyewitnesses as a large crowd. Shouting "Down with Fidel! Down with communism!", the crowd damaged or destroyed many of the patrol cars. The police had to call for Interior Ministry troops for reinforcement, and that is as far as my information reaches.

This is not an isolated incident. The end is near. On August 27, 1993, in the town of San Miguel del Padron, three policemen were injured by bottles filled with sand thrown at them. A few days before, on August 24, a guard post at the entrance to the military base Ciudad Libertad had been attacked by bottles, and on August 22, at the Puente de la Lisa, bottles were thrown at vehicles. *The Miami Herald* reported that in mid-August 1993, a pitched battle developed in the area of Havana called Santos Suarez, lasting about two hours and involving a reported one thousand people. It ended when government trucks brought scores of thugs armed with chains and iron bars to beat up the demonstrators.

Sabotage is increasing. In the coastal town of Cojimar, in late August 1993, a deliberately set fire destroyed one hundred fifty storage sheds used in the fishing industry. Cojimar had become famous because a few weeks earlier, government border guards shot and killed three people trying to leave the island on boats that had been sent from Florida. The townspeople who witnessed the killings attacked the border guards, who retreated and asked for help from Ministry of Interior troops. In every case, anti-Castro and anti-communist slogans are heard and the following morning seen painted on the walls until removed by the neighborhood vigilance committees.

This venting of emotion in such an unsightly manner may be explained by the deterioration of economic conditions, by the weight of thirty-four years of inability to express one's most basic emotions, and perhaps by a little-known phenomenon — "tourism apartheid." Tourism apartheid refers to the official Cuban government policy of physically prohibiting the entry of any unauthorized Cuban citizen into a tourist hotel, beach, or other facility. Imagine, if you will, if Canadian citizens were physically barred by Canadian police from entering the hotel where we are meeting now, a national park, or any other installation where only foreigners with hard currency were allowed. This has been the policy of the government of Cuba, and it has created understandable resentments.

Recently, a U.S. journalist who frequently visits Cuba returned with a story that would be funny if it were not true. He tells that a small group of Cuban children spotted him as a foreigner and quickly struck up a conversation. They asked him if he had any candy or chewing gum or anything else to give them. He gave them whatever he had in his pocket, and then he asked what many of us have asked numerous times of ten-year-old children: "What do you want to be when you grow up?" He expected to hear the usual "fireman" or "architect" or "doctor." The answer he heard more than any other from this group of children of the revolution was that when they grow up they want to be a "foreigner" or a "tourist." After all, children learn early that in Cuba today, in addition to the Communist party nomenclatura, only foreigners and tourists eat well and are treated with a modicum of decency.

But there are indications that the end is near. The numbers of so-called boat or raft people — those who set out to brave the Florida Straits separating Cuba from the United States — are at an all-time high. In 1983, fewer than one hundred people so risked their lives; today they come at the rate of twenty-five hundred per year. Most of them do not make it to land. It is estimated that only one out of every four is able to survive the journey of inner tubes or planks tied together with rope and covered with burlap (pitiful vehicles such as those exhibited recently in Washington by Freedom House, an organization that has been opposing dictatorships since 1941).

Imagine the conditions that must prevail in Cuba to cause a human being to enter an inner tube raft and cross shark-infested waters, often tossed by tropical storms, to go to a foreign country with no assurance of survival during or after the voyage. It is easy to talk in terms of statistics and to speculate as to what proportion of the Cuban people still support the government. If anyone is interested in attaching names to these statistics, several human rights organizations would be happy to show you the names and faces of some of those who survived the crossing and, unfortunately, some of those who did not. These people are ordinary Cubans. They are, almost without exception, of the age group either to have been born or have come to age during the revolution. They all know there is something very important missing from their lives: liberty. That is the first thing that they celebrate if they make it ashore.

Perhaps as a result of this (having created a society in which ordinary Cubans are second-class citizens), on July 26, 1993, Castro announced a change in policy regarding foreign exchange. Cubans who heretofore would have been jailed for holding dollars, francs, marks, or any other hard currency, would be allowed to traffic in those despised capitalist currencies. It is not yet clear what impact this change will have on the second-class citizenship of the Cuban people in their own country vis-à-vis foreign tourists. The memories of humiliation, however, will not easily be dismissed by presidential decree.

Not too long ago, a Cuban woman who now lives in Miami told the story of walking down a Cuban beach with her 8-year-old son on a hot day. She was on holiday from her government job (all jobs in Cuba are government jobs), and like most Cubans, lacking any real diversion from the drudgery of everyday life in a country where every single aspect of national life is rationed by the state, she decided to take her son swimming. She brought along a plastic bottle filled with drinking water, knowing that it was going to be very hot at the beach. Her son accidentally dropped the water bottle, and the water spilled onto the sand. Naturally, about an hour later, they were both thirsty. Walking down the beach, she approached the outdoor restaurant of a fashionable foreign-operated tourist hotel and asked a waiter for a glass of water for her son. The waiter quickly looked very sad and upset. Lowering his voice, he apologetically asked the woman to leave because, he said to her, "Look over my shoulder, do you see the man in the corner? If he sees me giving you a glass of water, I will lose my job, and you will not get your water. So please do us both a favor and leave."

This kind of shameful story has been repeated countless times in many different ways and has contributed increasingly to the Cuban people's resentment toward foreign visitors, a resentment that never existed before. The only other time they harbored such sentiments was thirty-five years ago, when Havana hotels had gambling operations controlled by persons alleged or known to be with organized crime. Many Cubans strongly resented those who ran illegal activities at that time, but now tourists are the targets of their resentment.

It was no surprise that on January 1, 1959, when the Batista dictatorship suddenly disappeared, large and unruly mobs vented their resentment and frustration at the gambling casinos, which, in their view, embodied corruption and financial support for the dictatorship that had oppressed them. As a 14-year-old boy, I witnessed that cathartic shudder of violence as my family and I drove around the streets of Havana.

We wanted to see for ourselves the huge crowds celebrating the downfall of the Batista dictatorship that we had all despised. While the vast majority of people were simply happy and well-behaved, others took advantage of the breakdown of law to destroy anything associated with the previous order. We must wonder whether there will be a repetition of such spontaneous violence against the visible forms of financial support of the current dictatorship when it, too, comes to an end.

I mentioned ethics and morality as two of the factors that constitute problems — and should constitute obstacles — to investing in Cuba today. I realize that these factors very seldom enter into investment decisions. For five years in the 1970s, I was director of Washington operations of the Council of the Americas, the association of the two hundred largest U.S. corporations with investments in Latin America, so I know which criteria are more prevalent in deciding investments. Fortunately, however, more and more ethical and moral considerations, such as labor conditions and respect for human rights and the environment, are factors being considered by the more socially conscious investors.

For these reasons alone, no self-respecting corporate executive should consider doing business in Cuba. According to the International Labor Organization (ILO), Cuba is guilty of official forced labor. Thus, Castro joins a select group, including Hitler, Stalin, and Mussolini, as leader of a country in which forced labor officially exists outside prison. The ILO further finds the Cuban labor force works excessive hours, is subject to the militarization of labor, and suffers from other characteristics which have been described as a Stalinist model of collective labor relations.

Labor unions in Cuba are not independent and autonomous, as they are in democratic societies. Labor leaders, as well as managers of enterprises, are subservient to the will and whims of the party and the government. There is no freedom of association — you must belong to a union if you want to work in Cuba, and it is controlled by the state. Anyone who tries to establish an independent trade union is accused of undermining the state and punished severely. No repetition of the Polish "Solidarnosc" experience will be tolerated. No matter what face the government tries to put on in order to entice either naive or greedy investors, all must keep in mind that the labor they will be using in any Cuban enterprise is based on involuntary labor. Ask yourself the question, "What would a Canadian worker do under these circumstances?"

In answer to that question, some people say, "Well, if the Cubans are so unhappy, why don't they just rebel?" One answer was provided by the head of counterintelligence of the Soviet KGB, General Oleg Kalugin, to a visiting American delegation in Moscow about two years ago. When the topic turned to Cuba, one of the Americans asked the same question: "Why don't the Cubans rebel?" The Russian general replied, "Because Castro has the best security apparatus we have ever seen, much more efficient than ours ever was." But as we saw earlier, there is evidence that among many Cubans the fear is gone, and if so, the end of Castro's regime is near.

Perhaps it is practical to invest in Cuba. Perhaps there is money to be made. But is it right to help a dictatorship? On the very day that the Gulf War started, January 16, 1991, President Bush asked me to represent the United States before the UN Human Rights Commission in Geneva. In the State Department I had not been an expert on human rights, and on that day as I watched the bombing of Baghdad on television, I was not particularly anxious to find out if the threats of

Arab terrorist groups against U.S. property were true, preferring to stay on the safer side of the Atlantic Ocean.

I had left government service more than a year before and was trying to establish myself in a highly competitive consulting business. I felt a little bit like the inexperienced football player who is asked by the coach late in the fourth quarter to go into the game and substitute for a star player. Before the inexperienced player is able to feel too good about possibly being the game saver, the coach says, "Quick, kid, we're out of time-outs — get in there and get hurt."

When the president of the United States asks you to undertake a mission of this sort, especially in the middle of an armed conflict, you have to answer "yes." So I went to Geneva and worked with a slimmed-down but very dedicated U.S. delegation. With the unwavering support of the Western democracies — and I am proud to say, including the Canadian delegation — the U.N. Human Rights Commission singled out for condemnation such clear and consistent violators of human rights as Iraq, Iran, Cuba, and others. In that session, we even managed to point the spotlight of international attention on violations of human rights in China and what was then still the Soviet Union.

That session, which ended in March 1991, resulted in the highest condemnation of human rights violations in Cuba's history before the Commission. The UN appointed a special rapporteur to investigate and catalogue thousands of human rights violations, the same treatment accorded in the past, among others, to Chile under Pinochet, Guatemala under the generals, Afghanistan under Najibullah, and Iraq under Hussein.

This illustrates the extent of world disapproval for the internal conditions in Cuba today. In the resolution that condemned Cuba and called for this special rapporteur, and which, by the way, has been repeated in 1992 and 1993, the only countries voting with Cuba were Syria, Iran, Iraq, China, Somalia, and the then-USSR. (Russia has since voted in favor of the resolution condemning Cuba's human rights violations.) This gives you an idea of the regimes that feel comfortable defending Castro.

We were proud to have all the former East European states on the side of condemning the Castro regime. They had suffered for nearly fifty years under communism. Prior to the fall of the Berlin Wall, Castro's closest ties had been with some of the bloodiest dictators on the other side of the Iron Curtain.

Just a few days before the overthrow and subsequent execution of Nicolae Ceausescu in Romania, Castro sent one of his most trusted lieutenants to express the Cuban government's solidarity with the enlightened leadership of President Ceausescu. Perhaps it is this side of the ideological and personal association with Ceausescu which has led many to fear a "Romanian scenario" in Cuba — rather than a more peaceful Czech or Hungarian-style transition out of communism.

Throughout the 1970s and 1980s, Romania was characterized as one of the most open and pro-Western of the communist countries. One evidence was its openness to trade. President Ceausescu was portrayed as an enlightened, if autocratic, ruler who was trying to lead his country beyond the traditional backwardness of the Iron Curtain. Even U.S. President Ford believed the story and actually danced in the streets of Bucharest with Comrade Nicolae. Ceausescu himself had no reason to doubt his popularity. After all, the adoring crowds loyally presented themselves at the presidential rallies where they would listen and cheer the maximum leader, or whatever the Romanian equivalent of "Fuhrer" is.

The Romanian charade continued until one fateful day in December 1989, when the adoring crowds could not hide the truth and the hate any longer and began a violent convulsion, which in a few days would cost the lives of Ceausescu, his wife, and many of their henchmen but, more important, would expose, one more time, as if we needed it, the immense cruelty of totalitarian communism, a cruelty for which Romanian children are paying even to this day, and because all of you have seen it so often on television I do not have to recount it. But why do we not learn from these lessons?

In Cuba after thirty-five years of a closed society, no press freedom, and total control of all means of communication, association, and production by one man and one political party, does anyone here know what secrets are going to be unearthed? Will we see the inside of the Cuban Gulags denounced by every human rights group in the world? Will we see the ecological devastation in East Germany and Russia? Will we find mass graves and examples of other atrocities? If they have been found in every other country where a communist government ruled, will we not find them in Cuba as well? There are already indications that, unfortunately, we will.

The time has come for thirty-five years of dictatorship by one man in Cuba to come to an end. The suffering chronicled by the UN and by dozens of human rights organizations around the world must come to an end soon. The joke in Cuba is that the government has already fallen but is caught up in bureaucratic red tape. The oldest military dictatorship in this hemisphere is on artificial life support. It is time to pull the plug.

It is important that Castro's downfall be transparent, that it not be influenced by events from abroad. As Latin American, Asian, and African nations discard the failed socialist systems that have bankrupted their economies and abolished their political freedoms, it is important that the Castro experiment be seen for what it is and has been — a colossal failure.

Those who say that the embargo on Cuba should be lifted ignore the impact of embargoes on countries such as Chile, Haiti, and South Africa. No one really knows what the people of Cuba think. For one thing, public opinion polls are not allowed because the government fears the public's opinion.

It is not the U.S. embargo which causes these people to risk their lives. It is the abject failure of the government of Cuba to provide for the most basic human needs — a government headed by a most selfish and stubborn individual who was never chosen in any free election, who has become a "historical curiosity" (those are the words of *The New York Times,* not my own), and who stands as the only obstacle between the revival of what was once the second-most prosperous economy in Latin America and what will once again be a vibrant economy.

I believe it is immoral to lengthen the days in which an undemocratic, brutal, unelected, totalitarian regime survives to imprison, torture, execute, and cause to flee more innocent people. There have always been people willing to benefit from the suffering of others. There have always been people who rationalized doing business with unsavory characters. Those who insist on dealing with Castro ignore seventy years of communist history. They do so at their own moral and financial peril.

# BUSINESS PERSPECTIVE ON INVESTMENTS IN CUBA

## Alberto Luzarraga

A nalyzing foreign investments in Cuba as a businessman and a banker, I conclude that the Cuban government may be conducting a "fire sale of its assets" and that foreign investors should be careful about leasing or purchasing properties in which former owners may have a claim. In addition I caution that investors may be paying below market prices for these properties thus increasing the possibility of a backlash by future governments. These governments may either seek higher compensations or disallow these transactions altogether.

The other key problem is that of nationalistic reactions. If major properties are sold or leased to foreign investors, Cubans may react negatively to their country being "sold out" to foreigners. Pressures on the present and future regimes will result in policies restricting foreign investments and their operations in the island. Increased regulations and taxation may result, making these investments less profitable.

Our task is to analyze investments in present day Cuba from a business standpoint. Let us then try to think — like a business person or entity making such an investment. Initially, this hypothetical person or entity may say the following:

- Capital knows no borders and flows naturally to those places where conditions are most favorable.

Alberto Luzarraga joined Continental Bank as senior vice president and group head of Latin America International Banking in 1986 and became managing director of the corporation in 1989. Dr. Luzarraga is a member of the Advisory Board of the Council of the Americas and of the Spanish-American Institute.

- Transactions concluded with sovereign governments have a certain mantle of protection, as the successor governments are bound to recognize the fait accompli.

- We are entitled to a good price and a quick payback since, after all, we are entering at a bad economic moment and change lurks in the horizon.

## *Analysis of the Thought Process*

1. It is true that capital is essentially return and conditions oriented, but it is not true that it is or should be oblivious to profoundly disturbing internal conditions. Throughout the Cold War, the Western countries in an overwhelming majority refrained from investments in COMECON countries, mostly due to their own policies. In the case of South Africa, many investors exited the country or refrained from investment. Setting aside the issue of the merits of any such policy, it is obvious that the "favorable conditions" argument has a substantial historical precedent against it.

If favorable conditions are granted by a regime that is out of step with commonly accepted juridical and political principles, including transparency and citizens' rights, such an investment of its own accord acquires a mechanistic patina wherein the main observable element is the desire to obtain the maximum profit in the minimum time. All other considerations are then deemed to be secondary. It is submitted that this is a very short-sighted and narrow approach that is bound to cause future problems. In fact, in certain instances it may put the investor in a nearly indefensible position, simply because public opinion at some point is bound to turn against him and turn with considerable passion.

2. The point that successor governments are bound by prior acts is valid in general political theory. However, it is not an absolute principle, and history is replete with examples of invalidation of previous acts. The Cuban Revolution itself is an example; it confiscated American-owned property, and now it is willing to discuss compensation. But our real business point has to do mainly with what are commonly accepted procedures to negotiate and price a transaction.

In any of the recent privatization processes in Latin America, France, Great Britain, or other countries, matters have been handled *professionally,* meaning:

a. Independent appraisals are made.

b. An auction or a stock market placement is arranged.

c. A reasonable market price is realized.

d. Due diligence is exercised vis-à-vis existing or hidden liabilities with the view of obtaining a clean and unencumbered title.

Now then, a negotiation with a government conducting a "fire sale" without any transparency is the opposite of all of the above. It is quite doubtful that a person negotiating under privileged circumstances can claim later on that it was a third party in good faith, particularly if the price paid and conditions obtained are notoriously advantageous to the buyer and detrimental to the seller. Juridically there are legal remedies to correct such a situation post-fact without violating (indeed by simply enforcing) commonly accepted contractual principles existing in most Western law.

The issues of due diligence and prior rights are also very important. The press recently reported that the Hotel Habana Libre, formerly the Habana Hilton, had been "sold" to a Spanish investor. The problem is that the hotel used to belong to the pension fund of the Restaurant Workers Union. Yes, before Castro, Cuba had unions and advanced social legislation. Tourism was, is, and will continue to be a big industry in Cuba. There will again exist an independent and very important Restaurant Workers Union. They are entitled to a pension. Are we to expect that they will accept a pittance for a prime property situated on one of Havana's best corners? Shouldn't the union be able to lease the property, conduct an auction, or do whatever is economically most intelligent? Isn't this reasonable?

The alternative would be to suppose that one generation of workers left no legacy to another generation because of simple government fiat and that the present generation will accept this injustice passively while somebody else enjoys the fruits of their labors. Unfortunately, some investors have not bothered to do their social and historical homework. Contrary to the present government propaganda, Cuba was not a backward country in 1959, an educated middle class existed and now exists abroad, and there are corporate records and sufficient knowledge and resources to raise proper objections. In addition, since 1959, a great number of well-educated Cubans who live on the island have joined the middle class, perhaps not in economic terms but certainly in intellectual terms.

Thoughtful Cubans in both groups (inside and outside the island) recognize that there is a new sociopolitical reality in Cuba and that change is necessary. That the "status quo ante" cannot be reproduced is clear, but neither should it be absolutely ignored. In any case, both groups of thoughtful Cubans believe that the nation's assets cannot be spirited or practically given away by a bankrupt regime to the detriment of the whole society. Cuba must privatize, but it needs to obtain the best economic conditions as a result of this process.

The burning political issue of the future will be: Was the nation adequately compensated? If it was, it can take care of its present citizens and do justice (according to its means) to previous owners. Fair compensation is not the only major issue. Cuba must privatize in an open process that allows the present population to participate in an appropriate measure.

If, on the contrary, Cuba finds itself impoverished and in the hands of a few foreign investors who bought at "fire sale" prices, the reaction will be so negative that an investor will be placed in difficult circumstances. In sum, the argument of buying from a sovereign government is fraught with danger, both from a juridical and socioeconomic standpoint.

3. The argument of obtaining a very good price and a quick payback because the risk is high is really a double-edged sword. The investor seems to accept some degree of culpability and to mitigate the risk/fear equation that stipulates a quick payback. Strategically, it is the argument of a speculator rather than that of an investor who wishes to develop long-term roots in a market. Again, it puts the investor in a vulnerable position.

## Conclusion

Long-term business investors must look, and most often in fact do look, beyond the simple numerical values. A business is a living part of a community and a society. If this society is literate and educated, it will eventually become aware of its rights and the true worth of the elements of production and give cash, capital, labor, assets, and so on their proper valuation. This is the case in Cuba, with the added feature that the island's literate population can also count on a well-educated exile population that can bring it up to date instantly on what constitute normal business practices.

In the end, democratic governments must respond to public opinion. Gross injustices or evidently one-sided transactions will be publicized, analyzed, and inevitably changed or declared null and void. Such is the normal path of political-economic discourse.

Serious investors must ponder all of these factors and ask themselves when and whether they are prepared to face the above-mentioned issues. If they feel that the present undemocratic situation will endure without consequences during the life of the investment, then the decision to invest (moral issues notwithstanding) may be in the eyes of many selfish, but at least logically defensible; if they believe it will not endure for the life of the investment, they would be ill advised to disregard the obvious clouds gathering on the horizon.

# THE REALITIES OF INVESTING IN CUBA

Donald McQ. Shaver, Jr.

My acquaintance with Cuba and its people goes back several years. I can remember as a young boy having some Cubans stop at our farm in Cambridge, including one time a former revolutionary fighter who was holding a machine gun between his knees — these were very interesting people, and they provided very interesting company.

One of the prime goals of Fidel Castro has been to improve the lives of the average citizens of Cuba. At the time of the revolution the population of Cuba was around 5 million, and today it is about 11 million people. So in just over thirty years the population of Cuba has more than doubled, and, of course for export reasons, much of the prime land has gone over to sugar cane and tobacco. So the government has the responsibility for providing twice the amount of food as was required in the past, on a diminishing amount of land. Now this may change — with the loss of the Soviet and Eastern European markets, perhaps more of the prime land will be used for food production.

We in the agriculture business are very proud, and it is part of Canadian policy, of never having allowed politics to govern whom we deal with. We should never lose sight of the fact that it is people who are often innocent bystanders who can suffer as a result of conflicts between governments and regimes, as is all too apparent in the Balkans today.

Donald McQ. Shaver, Jr. is president and chief executive officer of D. McQ. Shaver Beef Breeding Farms Ltd. and D. McQ. Shaver Beef Breeding Farms International Ltd.

Basically, Castro has done a wonderful job of feeding the people of Cuba. Castro has his own farm, and I have visited it. He observed for himself that the Canadian Holsteins are not entirely adapted to the Cuban climate, so he has embarked on a project involving cross-breeding the Canadian Holstein with an indigenous breed of cattle. The project has been very successful, resulting in a very productive breed that does not require a lot of management and high-tech inputs.

Cuba really didn't have an organized poultry industry prior to the revolution. Typically, chickens ran in backyards of individual homes, where a family member gathered eggs and brought them to the local market. As a result of the U.S. boycott, our company had the unique opportunity of being the developer of the poultry industry in Cuba. In fact, today 90 percent of all poultry products in Cuba originated from Shaver poultry breeding stocks. (We also have developed poultry industries in Pakistan in a joint venture.) Significantly, the Cuban population has expanded on a finite chunk of land, and it appears that the pressures of maintaining exports for sugar and tobacco mean that a lot of food production is not taking place on Cuba's prime land.

I was approached in 1988 by a high-level Cuban mission to Canada and told that while Cuba required about 500,000 cattle for dairy production, it had a surplus of about 400,000 cattle that it wanted to streamline into a beef-producing animal that could provide high quality meat for the tourist trade. (Cuba is very interested in expanding its tourist industry. Right now tourists rave about Cuba's beautiful beaches and warm, sunny climate, but if you ask them how the food was, they reply that it wasn't so good.) Beef production is secondary to milk production, but Cubans recognize that if the tourist trade is going to expand significantly, they have to increase the volume of beef. Remember, while the beach and the sun are important to tourists, dining out is another essential form of entertainment, and, naturally, their expectations are fairly high in this regard.

In this presentation, I want to take a broad view at first and then a look back. At this time, my company has three joint ventures under way: we invested in Hungary in 1990 and in Australia and New Zealand in 1989 and 1990. I believe that North American business people have never had as many foreign investment opportunities as they do today. With the collapse of communism, areas such as the former Soviet Union, Eastern Europe, and China are all eager for foreign investment. The economic growth in the Pacific Rim also has strong appeal to investment-minded entrepreneurs. In short, we have the capital, the management skills, and the technology that is desperately needed in these emerging economies.

With so many investment opportunities, business people can be selective and drive a hard bargain. That means that you have to evaluate the areas you are planning to go into and do a complete "health check" on each country to see what the possibilities are for investment there. Generally speaking, if a country cannot offer the potential investor minimum assurances, that country is not yet ready for foreign investment. Potential investors should delay until they are able to find an investment environment compatible with their objectives. Your company's assets and technology have been acquired through hard work, diligence, and attention to detail. Do not expose all that you have worked so hard to establish to regimes where red tape, graft, and corruption can destroy any hope of achieving financial success.

With regard to Cuba, we have heard assurances from very high levels, but at this point I have not seen a sincere change of attitude, demonstrating that Cuba will welcome foreign investors with open arms. Don't forget that part of the reason that the revolution took place was because Castro felt, along with many of his comrades, that Cuba was losing ownership of Cuba. And I do think that there is a very sensitive point beyond which Cubans will not tolerate foreign ownership, so potential foreign investors must be sensitive to this. We have to find the balance of what is acceptable and what will work in reality.

## Reasons for Investing Abroad

Here are five very good reasons why business people would be interested in a foreign investment:

1. Before the collapse of communism, one reason for investment in an area may have been to represent free enterprise in sensitive areas that were susceptible to communist persuasion. Since the collapse of communism, this is no longer a good enough reason to invest in a region. Much of Africa and Latin America (including Cuba) once fell into this category.

2. You may wish to invest in a region where you or your relatives were born. This still has strong appeal. For example, there is a

large Hungarian Investment Fund in Budapest that is Canadian in origin. Many Hungarians living in Canada have invested in this fund, estimated to be in excess of $300 million.

3. Many investors look to invest in a country that has immense resources, population, and potential, both in the medium and long terms. China certainly would fall into this category.

4. You may wish to invest in a country that has a progressive government, a stable economy, and the potential for serving as the entry point for gaining access to a much larger market within that region, again in the medium to long terms. For our company, Hungary represented such an opportunity. After more than thirty years of formal business dealings, we estimated that Hungary could best offer potential access to Western Europe, Eastern Europe, and the former Soviet Union. It was stable and not in danger of splitting, unlike Yugoslavia and Czechoslovakia. Hungary had historical ties (the Austro-Hungarian Empire) with Western Europe and had traded heavily with the Soviet Union since 1945. In 1991, we formed a joint venture in Hungary with Babolna Kombinat, one of Hungary's premier agricultural companies.

5. The investment climate and opportunities at home may not be appealing. Taxes and regulations may be so cumbersome that entrepreneurs are being driven away. For example, it is becoming increasingly difficult to set up businesses in Canada because of environmental issues, tax issues, and so on. It is quite possible that business people in North America may seek to invest in an outside country because it offers lower levels of government interference.

It is reasonable to suppose you would want to make an investment first as a joint venture, which entails finding a joint venture partner. In many of the former communist countries, that is not easy to do. They have not had to exercise the discipline we have, and often they have been able to survive with less than acceptable management skills.

## The Realities of Investing in Cuba

By all accounts, Cuba is very poor. Without major financial assistance from the former Soviet Union, I doubt that it could have existed in isolation for so long. Since the collapse of communism, there has been much speculation about Cuba's future.

As free enterprise begins to come into countries like Cuba, further social dislocations can result. To illustrate: I have a veterinarian friend in Hungary who was managing a very productive farm there. One night, after she had been there for about six months, she was threatened at knife point by some men who said, "You're working us too hard, and we don't like it." She said that she realized very quickly that she had better back off or she might not be alive the next day.

Many socialist countries have never experienced high levels of unemployment. As free enterprise comes in, one of the very first changes to be made is to streamline the labor force substantially, and the people that have been let go feel betrayed. That's the case in Hungary now: unemployment is high, gasoline prices are at a premium, and you just don't leave your car unattended at night because people will come along and siphon the gas from it. Those are some of the unhappy results of free enterprise that we have to live with, along with rampant black marketing and other dislocations.

At this point, I have not seen in Cuba a major change in the official attitude toward foreign investment. Those in power have not offered entrepreneurs sufficient incentives to become involved in large-scale investment in Cuba. If foreign investment is to be made, there are some very important criteria that first must be met. All assets must be secured. This means that before a cent is spent on renovations or improvements, the buildings, factories, and land must become the property of the investor. Smart business people would realistically consider providing funds to improve assets that do not belong to them. In addition, it should be made clear that further land and holdings may be bought in the future, either from profits generated in Cuba or from further foreign investment. Profits should not be withheld. Companies have every right to expect to be able to repatriate profits from their off-shore enterprises.

All top level management positions should be filled by your own personnel for at least the first two years to establish procedures and a method of operation that is acceptable and compatible with the parent company. Accounting and financial reporting in countries such as Cuba are often not like those found in North American companies. Before setting up a company, either on your own or as a joint venture, ensure that accounting procedures and reporting formats are standardized and provide the information required. Also, be aware of any taxes that you may be in line for in the long term. We have discovered in Hungary that although there are low wages, the government charges a very high social insurance. In some cases, this tax is equal to as much as 40 percent of the original wage. This is mandatory and cannot be avoided. Be very careful in countries where government tax levies exist because these costs can spiral, and you have no control over them.

If local managers are to be utilized, a whole new attitude must be developed. Since there was no personal reward for increasing profits in the past, most managers are not profit driven. Efficiencies in the workplace were seldom rewarded financially. In most communist regimes, it is impossible to be fired, so there is a false sense that there will always be a job, regardless of how incompetent an employee is or how often he fails. Rewards and advancement must come from successes and a good track record.

The first entrepreneurs seldom have overwhelming success. It often takes time for both sides to make adjustments, both in terms of expectations and what is actually attainable. The early entrepreneurs break down barriers and taboos for later investors. Cuba will not be any different. I would say that investment in Hungary now is less of a risk than it was in 1991. The same is probably true of China. The first "Marco Polos" in China, generally, came away disillusioned and far short of their initial goals.

But when I look at Cuba, I don't see some of the key elements that are necessary to attract investment. My company is at the point where it has made some initial investment, but no long-term agreements have been signed. Right now, making long-term decisions would be very difficult since we don't know what the future is going to hold for Cuba. The Castro regime won't be there forever, and it is uncertain what its replacement will be. Generally, based on conversations I have had, I think that there are many strong professionals in Cuba eager to get on with the job, who realize that as communism has failed in the Soviet Union and East European countries, it will fail in Cuba, too. Now that the Soviet money and subsidies are gone and are never coming back, Cubans have to face reality — just as here in North America we have had to accept a great deal of foreign ownership. Cuba has to realize that to attract foreign investment there will have to be a certain selling off of assets.

How secure those assets are is another concern. This is what worries me right now in Cuba. I am prepared to go a certain way ideologically and philosophically; I would like to help feed the Cuban people. But I cannot do it as a free handout, and in terms of priorities of where I could deal or would like to deal, Cuba is fairly low on the list right now. Basically, I see a bankrupt country.

Cuba does not have a huge population. It is not a stepping stone to other markets in the region. It does not have vast natural resources. Cuba does have lovely, sandy beaches and a mild winter climate. Tourism is, perhaps, Cuba's brightest area of development. Coupled with tourism are all the accessories that must accompany a booming tourist trade: top-notch hotels and condominiums, restaurants, night clubs, entertainment, and sports; reliable transportation; and security for tourists. Tourism would create jobs in construction in the short term and in the service sector over the long term. Much of the land that had been devoted to sugar production could be transferred to agriculture specifically for increased domestic and tourist consumption. This would be an area that my company would be interested in only if all other conditions were met.

## Conclusion

Of all the countries with investment opportunities in the world today, Cuba is not at the top of the list. However, Canada has had a unique opportunity to establish relations with Cuba at a time when U.S. foreign policy was to boycott any form of trade with Cuba. In that sense, Canadian business people have a recent history of trade with Cuba.

Tourism is probably the most appealing area of development, provided that ownership of land, buildings, and assets by investors is not prevented.

Before Cuba becomes an attractive place to consider investment, the Cuban government will have to demonstrate to business people that they are welcome with open arms. The first ones in may not be the most successful ones. They may simply cause changes to take place.

# CANADA-CUBA TRADE RELATIONS: PROBLEMS AND PROSPECTS

## Allan Gotlieb

In a world of rapidly unfolding changes, there is a part of the globe of increasing interest to Canada and our business community — Cuba. I wish to address briefly some of the issues associated with doing business with Cuba.

Cuba is a country confronted with many challenges. The collapse of the Soviet Union has seen to that. No longer is this small Caribbean island capable of fending off the economic allure of the Western democracies. Cuba now beckons, with the Castro regime's desire for more open commercial relations with countries like Canada, a desire fueled by a desperate need for foreign currency, not democratic ideals.

I expect that for many, Cuba is a country whose future may bring to mind the reasonable and possible prospects of expanded trade and commercial opportunities. Yet, it is also a country whose future course is an enigma. The Cuba of today remains the Cuba of Fidel Castro. The Cuba of tomorrow is difficult, if not impossible, to predict.

Today, more than at any time in the past thirty years, we are seeing the signs of change in Castro's Cuba. Whether that means a return to the Cuba of yesterday, or a new, made-in-Cuba democratic revival in the future, remains to be seen. Cuba today could indeed be on the eve of another revolution. Thirty-four years after Castro took power, the Cuban Revolution is on the ropes. There exists a widespread consensus, even within Cuba, that the nation's economic and political position, domestically and internationally, is untenable in the long term.

---

Allan Gotlieb is chairman of Burson-Marsteller Canada.

The former communist bloc, the traditional ally of the Castro regime, has, like the Soviet Union itself, crumbled into the ash heap of history. Cuba stands alone, clinging to Marxism-Leninism, buffeted by the dismal results of the Marxist philosophy, by natural disasters, and by an intensified U.S. economic embargo. Even as reform of one kind or another is expected, there is no consensus on the direction Cuba may be taking. Castro, who admits his former intransigence, recently was forced to take the unusual, perhaps unprecedented, step of opening sectors of the economy to foreign investment. There are no signs, however, of a parallel political opening.

Let me be clear — I am no soothsayer. He who lives by the crystal ball ends up eating ground glass. My purpose at this time is not to predict the future or to eat ground glass, but to discuss the prospects and problems presented by Cuba for Canadian businesses, based upon the historical development of our political and economic relations with that country.

In order to place Canadian relations with Cuba in their proper context, a brief background on Cuba and its recent history will be given, paying close attention to Cuba's stormy relations with our common neighbor, the United States. Drawing upon these factual observations, I will outline what we may expect concerning trade and investment opportunities, irrespective of regime change. In light of a sober review of current conditions, it is evident that circumstances call for a cautious and informed approach to doing business with Cuba.

## Cuba's Revolution

Cuba's modern political history has been defined by two related and concurrent factors: the regime's close alignment and integration with the now defunct Soviet Union and its isolation from the West as a result of ongoing tensions with the United States.

Castro promised a nationalist revolution that would change the economic, political, and social structure of the island. He fulfilled his promise by turning Cuba into one of the most slavishly orthodox of socialist states.

## American Rejection

In the United States, the emergent Marxist character of Castro's government was perceived as a threat. In 1960, the Americans cut off Cuba's sugar quota and restricted most exports to the island. The White House finally broke diplomatic relations with Cuba in January 1961. In April 1961, the U.S. State Department sponsored the ill-fated invasion of Cuba by Cuban expatriates — the Bay of Pigs — which solidified Castro's popularity in Cuba. The United States then led the Organization of American States (OAS) to eject Cuba from its membership in January 1962, and most OAS members broke diplomatic relations with Cuba. Partly as a response to Cuba's nationalization of foreign assets, the United States imposed a full economic embargo in 1962.

The Cuban leadership responded to American pressure by establishing close ties with the Soviet Union, which nearly led to a nuclear confrontation later in 1962 during the Missile Crisis. Castro responded to Latin American censure by supporting insurgent movements throughout Latin America, which in turn caused the Americans to maintain and tighten the economic and political embargo they imposed on Cuba.

During the 1960s, Cuba's relations with the Soviet Union were consolidated, and the Cuban economy was even more fully integrated into the Soviet system of exchange. Cuba's impact in the region began to diminish as revolts waned. Subsequently, relations were normalized with many Latin American countries in the 1970s. A potential thaw with the United States, however, was shattered when Cuba entered the African theatre as a Soviet military proxy in 1976 and remained there for a decade or so. The 1980s brought renewed hostility with a U.S. administration that placed increased focus on Cuba's support for rebel movements, but, at least in the eyes of some, less emphasis on the root causes of rebellion in Central America.

## Canada's Approach to Cuba — Diplomacy

From the start, Canada's approach to Fidel Castro's government diverged markedly from the United States' longstanding powerful rejection. Other than Mexico, Canada was the only country in the Western Hemisphere to maintain full diplomatic relations with Cuba following its revolution, and Canada never disrupted relations. Canada did not go along when the United States broke relations in 1961; we were not a member of the OAS in 1962 when the body suspended Cuban membership or in 1964 when the OAS imposed a trade embargo. Nevertheless, Canada has consistently and clearly expressed deep concerns over democratic and human rights issues in Cuba. These concerns have not diminished as our trade relations with Cuba have expanded. Canada ended its bilateral aid program to Cuba in 1979 and discontinued non-governmental organization (NGO) aid in 1981, in view of the regime's refusal to initiate substantive political and economic reforms as well as its poor human rights record.

The Canadian secretary of state for External Affairs issued a statement calling upon Cuban authorities to stop harassing human rights workers. In 1992, Canada co-sponsored a resolution at the UN Commission on Human Rights, criticizing Cuba's human rights record. The secretary of state for External Affairs announced that Canada would contribute $1 million for emergency hurricane relief to Cuba, as requested by a UN agency, but neither Canadian bilateral aid nor NGO programs have resumed.

## Canada's Approach to Cuba — Trade

In contrast to the United States, Canada has maintained normal commercial relations with Cuba following the revolution and never followed the economic embargo imposed by the United States and its Latin American allies.

Canada has never subscribed to the philosophy that general commercial trade should be used as a weapon of diplomacy. We think it doesn't work. On its own initiative, however, Canada applied restrictions on the export of strategic goods to Cuba, following the list approved by NATO. Sensibly, our government did not permit the export of arms.

Canadian trade relations focused on selected fields, such as Cuban agriculture, fisheries, and tourism. Canada buys Cuban sugar, nickel, shellfish, tobacco products, and rum. Cuba buys Canadian food and food products, industrial raw materials, and occasionally equipment and capital goods, such as those related to telecommunications.

Total two-way trade rose a modest 12 percent from 1987 to 1992 (from $324 million to $369.1 million), although exports and imports have been going in opposite directions. Our exports to Cuba in 1992 dropped to $113 million, nearly 60 percent (58.6 percent) lower than in 1987 ($272.89 million). Concurrently, our imports from Cuba grew from $51.57 million in 1987 to $256.1 million in 1992, an increase of 400 percent.

Despite these problems, it is a little-known fact that Canada was Cuba's largest hard currency export market and fourth-largest source of imports in 1991. In addition, Canadians have made Cuba one of their favored holiday destinations. Of the 340,000 tourists Cuba received in 1990, 26 percent came from Canada. Approximately 130,000 Canadians visited Cuba in 1991, and they spent more than $85 million. Foreign capital has not been allowed into Cuba until recently, but Canadians are among the first investors exploring the possibilities. The potential exists for a significant Canadian investment presence.

However, our commercial flow naturally has been affected by the economic crisis in Cuba. A consistent Canadian trade surplus became a deficit in 1991, as a result of Cuba's lack of foreign exchange with which to purchase Canadian products. Canadian exporters are no doubt aware of these trends. The prospects for continuing and expanding trade relations are contingent upon the health of the Cuban economy. It is worthwhile to examine the island's economic plight.

## Cuba's Economic Collapse

Throughout its history, the Cuban economy has been driven by the production of sugar and other crops for export. Before 1960, most of these exports went to the United States. Since then, most of Cuba's trade was conducted with the communist bloc. Consequently, Cuba was effectively crippled by the loss of its trading partners in Eastern Europe, especially the USSR.

According to UN estimates, Cuba's gross national product (GNP) was, at US$20.9 billion in 1989, growing by a scant 1 percent annually. So dependent was Cuba's economic health on the communist bloc that more than 81 percent of its exports and 85 percent of its imports came from that single source. With the collapse of the communist bloc, Cuban trade with its former partners plunged to barely 7 percent of its former levels.

Many experts believe that Cuba's economy has declined by as

much as 40 percent since 1989. Not surprisingly, by Cuba's own official estimates, the country's GDP declined by 14 percent in 1992 alone to an estimated $20.3 billion, reducing per capita income to less than $1,800 and falling. All economic indicators illustrate the sharp decline. A few striking examples will illustrate this.

In 1988 Cuba's exports totalled $5.5 billion. They consisted, typically, of sugar, nickel, shellfish, and other cash crops. The USSR and East Germany together absorbed 75 percent of Cuba's total exports. In 1992, Cuban exports may have reached $2.8 billion, roughly a 50 percent drop in only four years. New markets for Cuban products, therefore, are desperately being sought.

Cuba's imports in 1988 amounted to $7.6 billion, and in 1989 they exceeded $8 billion. Cuba bought capital goods, industrial raw materials, food, and fuel. Over 85 percent of Cuban imports came from the USSR and its allies. During 1991, Cuba could only afford $2.2 billion in imports, a drop of 70 percent in less than two calendar years. In 1992, Cuba's imports reached only 60 percent of 1988 levels, and Western Europe was the largest source of imports.

Notwithstanding all of this, we have to acknowledge that the Cuban Communist Party, at least publicly, refuses to abandon the ideals of Marxist ideology. The regime maintains a firm commitment to central planning, regardless of its evident weaknesses. Fidel Castro has reaffirmed the revolution's principles of social equality and distribution of resources. These promises have a somewhat hollow ring, given the desperate conditions under which Cubans must struggle today — hardships, deprivation, and restrictions unprecedented since Castro took power, and perhaps never seen before in Cuba.

Conditions in Cuba have become so desperate that Castro told Cubans on July 27, 1993, that "appropriate foreign investment can exist" in Cuba's Revolution. This is a definite change in policy. Castro went on to identify specific sectors wherein his government would encourage investors. He stressed that Cuba needs hard currency in order to survive and must get it through any means available. Other measures announced were meant to free convertible foreign exchange — mostly U.S. dollars sent by expatriates in the United States or brought in by tourists.

## Cuba's Potential

Castro's July 27, 1993 speech followed a constitutional amendment last summer that defined "the legal basis for the safeguards of foreign investments in Cuba." Such pronouncements have stirred international investors interested in developing Cuba's considerable economic potential. This potential is present in a variety of sectors:

- One-half million tourists visited Cuba last year, and the government is seeking foreign capital and technology with which to expand tourism facilities. Substantial opportunities also exist for the supply of goods and services to the expanding tourism industry.

- Cuba also wants foreign capital for exploration and development of the island's mining and resources potential. There are European firms already involved in off-shore oil exploration, and others are signing exploration contracts.

- There are research and production facilities in Cuba generating advanced biotechnology and pharmaceutical products. The government sorely needs foreign partners to help market this industry worldwide. Some agricultural products also are in need of marketing.

- Cuba's infrastructure, not merely the tourist industry, is in need of rebuilding. The nation needs new or refurbished transportation, energy, and communication networks, most of which will be accomplished through foreign technology and supplies.

- The government in Cuba has made considerable investments in human resources, to an extent seldom found in developing countries, and nowhere else in the region. They have invested in training and education, important areas, I think. For obvious reasons, literacy and technological education are critical factors for economic expansion and for a productive labor force.

- Barter agreements (not involving hard currency) recently negotiated with the Russian Republic and other former allies should bolster the collapsing economy.

However, for this potential to be fulfilled, Cuba must somehow deal with the formidable obstacles to its development.

## *Cuba's Problems*

As a result of its overwhelming economic dependence upon the former communist bloc, Cuba is now bereft of foreign exchange for purchasing even basic necessities. Although Castro himself acknowledges that the problems brought on by the collapse of communism in Europe will take many years to solve, most analysts expect it will take a generation or more.

In addition, an off-season hurricane leveled the island in March 1993, damaging public buildings, transmission lines, and water supplies. The storm also destroyed large parts of Cuba's sugar and cash crops. Combined with a lack of fertilizer and farm machinery, the sugar crop predicted for 1993 is 40 percent, or about US $450 million, smaller than expected. The implications of this natural disaster for cash-starved Cuba are serious. Without some kind of viable economic activity, Cuba cannot sustain, much less expand, the tourism industry. Without tourism, Cuba may not obtain the foreign exchange it needs to sustain economic activity.

As I mentioned at the outset, the uncertain prospects of the nation's political future are deeply troubling. Cuba remains a one-party state without the least indication of democratic reform; there is no *glasnost* in Havana. In fact, there seems to be less tolerance for dissent from the besieged Cuban government. It has been reported that repression in Cuba has escalated as the economy has tumbled. Other critics of the regime believe that the level of repression has only become more visible as the crisis has intensified but has not fundamentally changed.

In brief, Cuba remains a political dinosaur on the world stage today. The Canadian Department of External Affairs, nevertheless, concludes that despite the troubles, "Castro remains very much in control." While the Castro regime appears in control for now, what will happen after Castro? To repeat, no one can really predict.

Beyond contemplating this question, it is of utmost importance for any party interested in Cuba's economic prospects to consider its unresolved conflicts with the United States. Tensions between Castro's government and the United States affect nearly all facets of everyday life in Cuba and lie at the heart of Cuba's unpredictable political future. Relations have deteriorated even though the Soviet Union has disappeared. Insofar as the United States is concerned, the Cold War is not over with Cuba. Now that the Soviet umbrella has vanished, the economic embargo that the United States imposed over thirty years ago is having a much greater impact on the Cuban economy.

The United States extends its sanctions internationally through a variety of means, some of them extraterritorial. Ships that dock in Cuba are banned from U.S. ports, subject to fines, and/or impounding. U.S. aid assistance is conditional on a government's commercial relations with Cuba, a policy that affects regional and developing countries' trade. International financial institutions that the United States can control block all loans for development in Cuba. The preferential tariff scheme for developing countries' products is denied for Cuban exports.

In addition, there are reported cases of direct, extra-legal pressure exerted by the United States against companies seeking Cuban business from Britain, Spain, Italy, Japan, Brazil, Argentina, India, and others. Since 1992, the United States has advised third country governments and companies to avoid investment in Cuba that may involve assets claimed by U.S. citizens. There are 5,911 unresolved American claims against Cuba's nationalization valued at U.S. $1.8 billion (1962 rate).

The latest American measure was enacted in October 1992, when the United States passed "The Cuban Democracy Act," known more commonly as the Torricelli Law, after Congressman Robert Torricelli (D-NJ), who introduced the bill. A key objective of the bill is to restrict U.S. subsidiaries in a third country, such as Canada, from having any transactions with Cuba. Similar problems of extraterritoriality arose for Canadian exports to Cuba as far back as the 1950s. Unfortunately, the Torricelli Law has presented the extraterritorial issue in a most acute form. Canada became affected directly by the tensions between Cuba and the United States.

## Canada — Caught in the Crossfire

The Canadian government was quick to respond to the Torricelli Law, which it quite rightly considered an infringement of our national sovereignty. In October 1992, the government of Canada passed an order under "The Foreign Extraterritorial Measures Act" as a direct response. The order forbids any firm domiciled in Canada, U.S. owned or not, from complying with the U.S. law.

Unfortunately, the Canadian order does not actually resolve —
cannot, it seems, actually resolve — the problem faced by a Canadian
subsidiary contemplating trade with Cuba: on the one hand, its parent
company is obliged by U.S. law to make the subsidiary observe the
boycott; on the other, the subsidiary is obliged by Canadian law to
ignore the U.S. law. The matter is evidently a Canada-U.S. trade irritant,
to be settled through high-level discussions between ourselves and the
Americans.

The Torricelli Law is not, as I have said, the first incident of its
kind. Our trade relations with the Cubans consistently, and unavoid-
ably, have come into the sphere of U.S. extraterritorial sanctions.
Despite our consistent effort to resist third parties who wish to
constrain trade and commercial initiatives of firms domiciled in
Canada, Canadian firms have to be aware of unabated U.S. efforts to
restrict third-party trade with Cuba.

In fact, Canadian companies have faced obstacles from the United
States even when disputes concerned humanitarian exports that were
already exempted from the OAS embargo. In the last several years,
before the Torricelli Law, a number of Canadian firms, most of them
subsidiaries of American companies, did not engage in trade with Cuba
for non-commercial reasons linked to the U.S. embargo. Some
incidents involved trade in refrigeration equipment (Lennox Canada),
electrical equipment (Square-D Canada), restaurant equipment (Robert Canada), and cellophane paper (Hercules Canada). The Canadian
Departments of External Affairs and International Trade reacted
directly to a 1991 incident in which Pepsi-Cola Canada in Montreal,
after consulting with its head office in the United States, refused to fill
an order that would be exported to Cuba.

In spite of our government's protective and supportive measures,
Canadian companies may still find themselves sideswiped by U.S.
partners or shareholders complying with the Torricelli Law. This is
precisely what occurred in the recent, well-publicized case of Gemini,
the Canadian electronic reservation system.

As most of you know, the Gemini system allows the Canadian
travel industry to make international travel bookings for Canadians
flying to foreign destinations. It accesses many of its international
routes by computer links through its U.S. partner, Covia. In June 1993,
Covia announced that, because of the Torricelli Law, it was cutting off
access to all flight information related to Cuba, whether from Canada,

Mexico, or other locations. The net result of this action by Covia was that Gemini, a Canadian reservation system, could no longer make travel arrangements to and from Cuba. As mentioned earlier, Canadians interested in joint ventures in Cuba must remain aware of the unresolved U.S. claims on assets nationalized by the Cubans after the revolution.

We have learned a number of lessons from Eastern Europe that may be applicable to Cuba in a non-communist future. We know that a collapsed, centrally planned economy will require a considerable period of adjustment before it can readily absorb Canadian products, whether capital or consumer goods. Unlike Canadian firms, the Cuban economy and its people are conditioned to planning and to restrictions and not to respond to market demands. Furthermore, collapsed production, even socialist production, means a lack of capital, domestic savings, personal income, and, therefore, a lack of consumption.

Finally, the issue of property rights and the validity of current ownership and investment is bound to come into question. The return to private property in the not too distant future means the return of previous owners and prior claims to ownership. This can wreak havoc with long-term investment plans drawn in conjunction with a state that assumed control of all assets.

## Conclusion

Cuba offers distinct assets and opportunities right in our own hemisphere. This was the reason why Cuba was considered by Americans as the jewel of the Caribbean, as their exclusive playground prior to Castro. Unlike the United States, Canada enjoys full commercial and diplomatic relations with Cuba. Canadians are respected in Cuba. As such, we are ideally placed to take advantage of economic opportunities as they become available, before our U.S. counterparts. Although some may disapprove, and some do disapprove, our relations with the People's Republic of China demonstrate that we can trade successfully with a regime whose questionable human rights practices we publicly censure. However, the outlook for stability is possibly even more tenuous for Cuba than for China.

Opportunities exist in Cuba for Canadian entrepreneurs, their presence is sought, and the prospects may prove rewarding in individual cases. At the same time, it is necessary to be sensitive to the problems faced by the current regime and to the fact that the likelihood of change can affect the position of present investment in Cuba.

The island's socialist, planned economy is in the midst of an unprecedented crisis; it probably suffered a mortal blow with the fall of communism in Europe. The economic reforms or openings that have been announced are limited in scope and have arisen from desperation and isolation, rather than by choice. Investors can hardly expect the same openness in business relations found in western democracies.

There is uncertainty regarding such fundamental questions as the future of the Cuban regime, the direction of change, the economic viability of the whole system, and, of course, the place of current foreign investment in the post-Castro era. Stability remains an elusive goal in Cuba's distant future, whether political, diplomatic, or economic.

However, these uncertainties do not negate the fact that there may be some advantages to being on the ground when the new Cuba takes shape. For certain Canadian businesses seeking a competitive edge over their U.S. counterparts, the Cuban market does present a unique opportunity. Many Canadian companies and industries, such as the mining industry, are busily exploring and ready to exploit that situation by entering into economic agreements with Cuba.

Canadian tourism remains the island's leading source of tourists and foreign currency and may present the best overall opportunities for Canadian business. Canadian manufacturers of electrical and plumbing equipment, not American-made goods, are supplying many of the new hotels located on Cuba's beaches. All of these are examples of Canadian footholds in Cuba.

Canada's maintenance of trade relations with Cuba in good times and bad, such as during the U.S. embargo, suggests that Canadians are reliable partners. Therefore, Canadian companies, unlike U.S. businesses, continue to have the chance to develop linkages, understanding, and experience necessary for successful commerce with Cuba. That Canadian advantage will be valuable no matter what post-Castro Cuba becomes.

A Cuban transformation of some kind is inevitable. There are also some emerging indications in the U.S. academic and business communities of a desired softening of the American sanctions, with some observers hoping this would prompt more reforms in Cuba. But for now, the Clinton administration is showing no signs of ending the embargo. Canadians wishing to join Cuba in investment, therefore, must be aware both of the potential that exists as well as the difficulties involved in these enterprises.

# THE EXPERIENCE OF EASTERN EUROPE: SEVEN LESSONS FOR CUBA[1]

Vendulka Kubalkova

*Life punishes those who are too late.*
—Gorbachev in Berlin, 1989

*Post-communist transformation will be as hard as trying to reconstitute the fish and a fish tank from the fish soup into which the years of communism made it.*
—East European and Russian joke

The making of the Soviet form of socialism and conversion of countries to the Soviet image had no historical precedent. Today, the reversal of this monumental exercise is similarly without precedent. Four years into this process, there is a fast-growing literature documenting the unfolding experience of the implosion of socialism. There is no clear pattern or model of this process: the removal of socialist *Gleichschaltung* brings into sharp relief the tremendous differences between the different parts of the former Soviet Socialist Empire. But if a single model of reversal has not appeared, there are still lessons to be learned, lessons that may assist those who study or prepare for the final implosion of the few remaining socialist countries.

This paper examines those lessons that are particularly relevant for persons or organizations interested in the issue of investment in

Vendulka Kubalkova is professor of international relations at the Graduate School of International Studies, University of Miami.

one of those remaining socialist countries, Cuba. While the stress in the paper is on foreign economic relations, this should not be taken to suggest that the features of domestic reform are separable from the foreign issues of lesser importance.

I can identify at least these lessons:

- Lesson 1: Socialism always fails.
- Lesson 2: The legacy of failed socialism is enduring, the result of years of conscious and systematic efforts of socialist leaders and Cold War policies.
- Lesson 3: Reforms of socialism fail.
- Lesson 4: Reforms of socialism should not be confused with the abandonment or replacement of socialism.
- Lesson 5: Western foreign economic policies produce different outcomes if applied to reforming socialist economies, economies that have abandoned socialism but not yet instituted a new system, and economies where socialism has been replaced with a new (capitalist) model.
- Lesson 6: The role of foreign economic relations in influencing the collapse of socialism and assisting the post-socialist transition should not be overstated.
- Lesson 7: Based on the historical record, the collapse of Soviet-style socialism where it still endures should be anticipated, but the timing and form of that collapse is not predictable. The only certainty is that the post-socialist transformation will be extremely difficult and painful.

In the balance of this paper I will discuss each of these lessons: I do not attempt to extend these to Cuba, except in conclusion, in the form of two tentatively formulated final points.

## Lesson 1: Socialism always fails.

Socialism, invented as an antithesis to capitalism, was supposed to overcome capitalism's excesses and weaknesses. The variants of "realized" or "real" socialism (as the East Germans referred to existing forms of socialism) were based on different mixes of social ownership (private property in capitalism), economic planning (capitalist market), equality and participation in decision making (the inequalities and hierarchical political structures based on capital and profit). The rather narrow spectrum of political systems capable of implementing these economic elements, namely dictatorship, totalitarianism, authoritarianism, or neoauthoritarianism, are also antithetical to the Western forms of democracy normally accompanying capitalism.

Socialism came in several models designed for differing conditions. The "best selling" form of socialism,[2] generally referred to in the West as "communism," is the Stalinist model, conceived in the Soviet Union, reproduced in East Europe, and inflicted on a few non-European states. At the height of its spread, upward of twenty countries could properly be described as Stalinist socialist states. Among the Stalinist socialist countries there existed variations, reflecting the different initial endowments of the individual country as well as the manner of adoption of the model, in other words, the form of incorporation into the Soviet bloc. These differences now obtrude in the process of reversal of socialism.

But the Stalinist model was not the only variant available to socialists. There were other, cheaper models of socialism for the poor and specially adapted models for Third World development and modernization. While it lasted the self-styled Yugoslav model, based on the idea of cooperatives, attracted considerable attention. The non-Marxist Swedish model, touted as suitable for the rich West European countries, was the "Rolls Royce of socialism."[3] This was to be the "capitalism with a human face" model, the improved version of capitalism. It stood for collectivization not of private property but of private risk for both rich and poor. It respected private property but boasted a large nationalized sector, egalitarianism produced via progressive taxation, generous redistributive policies, large public consumption with ample provisions for social insurance, and central economic direction. In this type of socialism, it was theorized, public property and the state would play a prevailing and privileged role rather than receiving the equal treatment accorded to all sectors and forms of property in full fledged, multi-sectoral, capitalist market systems. Socialist reformers often suggested that Sweden offered a "third way," a model that would allow the transformation of centrally planned economies into "socialist market" economies or "social market" economies. Though this model had only a short life where it was fully applied ( Sweden), partially implemented (in Britain, Spain, France, Italy, and Australia), or adapted by Eurocommunist movements, the importance of the model lies in its long-term allure for East European liberal communist and post-communist leaders. The Swedish model will continue to lure the former communist states, despite its failure in the West. The problem is that like its namesake, Rolls Royce socialism is suitable only for the wealthy, and, because of the expenses associated with its operation and maintenance, tends to lead its owners toward bankruptcy.

The Swedish experience is relevant for post-socialist countries also because many of the transforming post-communist societies might get bogged down, *faut de mieux*, in a poor version of the Swedish model, incapable of reducing the privileged role of the state sector.

Socialism failed in all countries practicing it. Some of these former socialist states no longer exist and metamorphosed into several smaller states, frequently hostile to each other. Wars and civil wars rage in the former Yugoslavia and parts of the former Soviet Union. Other states abandoned socialism in revolutions that ranged from the violent (Romania) to the velvet (Czechoslovakia). Today "former socialist countries" find themselves heading away from socialism, on different points of post-communist transformation. They share incredible, possibly intractable, problems and devastation more far-reaching than statistics released before socialism's collapse indicated. Years of communism left behind seriously distorted and devastated economic structures, environmental wastelands, and totally demoralized populations.

Not only has the Union of the Soviet Socialist Republic ceased to exist, but so has its military alliance, the Warsaw Pact, and its economic organization, the Council for Mutual Economic Assistance (CMEA). The roll call of countries that a few years ago styled themselves as socialist[4] is now a list of countries of failed socialism and a sad indictment of the fate of socialism on this planet. Among the Marxist socialist countries, the roll call may be divided into five distinct categories.

Group One consisted of those socialist countries that were full members of the Council for Mutual Economic Assistance (CMEA). The CMEA itself was subdivided into the "core" (Bulgaria, Hungary, Romania, East Germany, Poland, and Czechoslovakia; and Romania, which maintained a degree of independence in foreign policy) and the non-European members, Mongolia, Cuba, and Vietnam.

Group Two were socialist countries whose relationship to the USSR fluctuated, who were not members of the CMEA, and who managed to remain outside Soviet domination: Albania, China, North Korea, and Yugoslavia.

Group Three were the countries of the communist Third World, countries that voluntarily proclaimed themselves Marxist-Leninist, sought membership in the CMEA, and received substantial aid from the USSR: Angola, Mozambique, the Peoples Democratic Republic of Yemen, Ethiopia, Afghanistan (before and during the Soviet occupation), Laos, Cambodia, Grenada, and Nicaragua.

Group Four consisted of "doubtful" cases such as Madagascar, Benin, Congo-Brazaville, Guyana, and Somalia whose development suggested they were heading toward membership in group two or group three.

The epicenter of this gathering, the Soviet superpower, was a "group" of its own. Today, the former Soviet Union is a disaggregated collection of fifteen separate states.

Today socialism survives in a near-bankrupt, heavily compromised form in pockets of the former Soviet Union, in Cuba, and in China. In all cases surviving socialism is propped up by heavy doses of capitalism.

## *Lesson 2: The legacy of failed socialism is enduring, the result of years of conscious and systematic efforts of socialist leaders and Cold War policies.*

Like the transformation of the aquarium into a bowl of fish soup and back to an aquarium, the unmaking of socialism will be almost too hard to imagine. It is useful to remind ourselves that a basic tenet of socialism at the time of its introduction was the need to make it irreversible. The stated intention of the socialist leaders was to create a self-imposed isolation from the capitalist system. According to Marxist-Leninist theory, the formation of socialism in one country and, in due course, the creation of a separate Eastern economic bloc would deepen the crisis of world capitalism and speed its inevitable demise. Denying communist markets to the capitalists was supposed to decrease capitalist exports, thus creating idle industrial capacity which would contribute to the economic and political collapse of capitalism.

The formation of a separate socialist bloc would insulate the socialists from the coming capitalist economic chaos and would enhance socialist economic development. Additionally, the USSR had a geostrategic goal: the creation of a buffer zone to protect it from its "natural enemy," the capitalist countries of the West. By its dominance over East Europe the USSR also obtained access on favorable terms to the resources of Eastern Europe — raw materials and capital equipment — that could be used to rebuild the Soviet Union after World War II and to advance its economic development.

By means of wartime diplomacy, postwar military occupation, and Soviet-instigated coups d' état, the USSR established the bloc and buffer it sought. The bloc/buffer states all underwent what was intended to be an irreversible process of adoption of the Soviet model of socialism. In this process, admission to the CMEA served as the "final vows" of loyalty to the socialist camp. Economies of Eastern European states were totally restructured to minimize their contacts with the West. Neither the Soviet Union nor the East European countries joined the new international institutions created after World War II by the West. East European countries that were under Soviet control immediately after the war were not allowed to join; those that joined before becoming bloc/buffer states were forced to pull out.[5]

Through the CMEA and a series of bilateral trade agreements between the USSR and East European countries, Eastern European trade was brutally redirected from West to East.[6] Also under Soviet pressure, financial ties were redirected from West to East. In many cases this severed long-standing links and traditions. East European currencies were made inconvertible. Foreign investment was nationalized and flows of private capital halted. Credit financing and credit were limited to purchase of raw materials and equipment from the Soviet Union.

Throughout the Cold War, East-West economic intercourse was minimal. This was a result of efforts not only by the Soviet Union but also the West. The self-imposed isolation of the bloc was heightened by the West's policy of denying to the Soviet Union and its allies economic resources that would enhance their military capability and political power. The United States in particular did its best to keep the East economically isolated. The opening of the economic front of the Cold War came with the passage of the U.S. Export Control Act of 1949. The United States also used the Johnson Debt Default Act of 1934 to deny financial resources to the East.[7] Another form of economic warfare was to deny the East access to Western markets, as in the 1951 Trade Agreement Extension Act, which withdrew all trade concessions to the countries of the Soviet bloc. As a result, products from the East were subject to the onerous Smoot-Hawley tariffs. The United States sought with mixed success to persuade other Western countries to impose similarly strict embargoes. In 1949 under the United States' pressure, the Coordinating Committee (COCOM) was set up to discuss and coordinate Western strategic embargo lists. NATO countries other than the United States did not restrict Eastern access to credit, and an effort by the United States to impose restrictions through international agreement failed. Nonetheless, by the 1950s, East-West trade was lower than in 1937. The Iron Curtain became not only political, ideological, and military but also economic.

In the early stages of the Cold War economic intercourse between the Soviet bloc and the capitalist West was restricted to minimal trade, unimportant either as a percentage of world trade or the total trade of East or West.[8] Under the Stalinist state monopoly on foreign trade, trading relations were conducted through state import-export companies. The goal of this arrangement was the total separation of foreign and domestic economic spheres and cushioning effects of capitalist economies on the socialist ones.

## Lesson 3: Reforms of socialism fail.

For a relatively short while the Soviet system appeared to be working, at least in the Soviet Union: it facilitated the industrialization of a backward country, financed a massive buildup of military power and victory in war, produced impressive (although short-lived) improvements in standards of education, health, consumption, employment, price stability, and scientific development.

In spite of a massive accumulation of capital and desperate efforts at integration of the CMEA economies, the signs of decay appeared by the mid-1950s. Reasons cited for the decay include demographic slowdown, exhaustion of labor reserves, and increasing cost of tapping natural resources. The drawbacks of the Soviet-type model were more quickly apparent and of greater impact in the countries of East Europe, countries that prior to World War II had achieved higher levels of economic development, social diversity, and democracy than had ever been the case in the USSR or its predecessor Russian Empire.

Paradoxically, the causes of the undoing of the socialist model were those Marx had predicted would cause the collapse of capitalism: a drive to accumulate, imbalances between means of production and consumption and in the investment cycle, and the tendency for the rate of profit and growth to fall. Instead of the chronic underinvestment and unemployment of labor which Marx foresaw in capitalism, socialism produced chronic overinvestment and unemployment of capital. As Nuti summarized it, "[t]he whole system is stuck in low gear, working at high revs without picking up enough speed after initial acceleration, the engine wastes fuel, overheats and . . . breaks down." Economic reform on its own can do little to correct these defects. The solution can only be political.[9]

It took the Soviets more than seventy years to figure this out. The history of socialism is replete with attempts at reform, reforms that sought to fine-tune socialism without altering its substance. In the last thirty-five years, numerous reforms intended to salvage the Soviet model were attempted: the 1957 Soviet model of regional decentralization; the East German sectoral decentralization model, and more generalized decentralizations (Lange) attempted in Poland; in Czechoslovakia (Sik/Dubcek); and also in the Soviet Union (Lieberman/ Kosygin reform). In Hungary, the "New Economic Mechanism" reform was introduced in 1968. Both Poles and Hungarians, far ahead of the rest of the Soviet bloc, moved in the seventies and eighties toward genuine market economy reforms. The final attempt to "fix the system" was Gorbachev's ill-famed *perestroika*.

All of these reform attempts sought, unsuccessfully, to come to grips with socialism's basic flaw, its view of the whole economy as a single giant firm, partitioned into sectors connecting individual enterprises to the central planning agency. The idea here is the famous substitution of capitalist "perfect competition" by "perfect computation" from the planners.[10] In theory it seems possible to replace the market, the social mechanism for solving millions of economic equations, with central planning. In reality the replacement does not work. Recognition of this basic reality led to reforms featuring decentralization, with the goal of injecting market elements into central planning without touching the framework of centrally planned economy. But the recognition of this reality was a classic example of "too little, too late." By the 1980s, economic problems throughout the

Soviet bloc reached critical proportions. CMEA countries' growth rates declined from an average of 6 percent per year in the 1950s to about 4 percent in the early 1970s, and, by the early 1980s, growth had fallen to 1 or 2 percent.[11]

The acknowledgment of economic problems that could not be resolved internally by the socialist countries triggered a reversal of autarchic attitudes toward the West. Forging foreign economic relations with the West and reliance on trade with the West became the new panaceas, as the rulers of the socialist countries struggled to avoid more costly or impossible domestic economic reforms. After the death of Stalin in 1953, East-West trade increased; from 1953 to 1958, Eastern exports to the West doubled; and from 1958 to 1962, they nearly doubled again. With the 1959-1965 Seven Year Plan, the Soviet Union acknowledged explicitly that it sought to alleviate some economic problems by acquiring Western technology.

In the early 1970s, when the USSR achieved equality with the United States in strategic weapons, the USSR began to view the West with more confidence and actively sought to import western technology and machinery; at the same time it developed an increasing dependence on the West for foodstuff. Socialist countries began to accumulate foreign debt.

Gorbachev's *perestroika* — restructuring — was predicated on "interdependence" with the West. East Europeans often joked about *perestroika*. In the past, reform had meant no more than shaking the same rusty screws in the same rusty socialist tin can. Under *perestroika*, shiny capitalist screws had been thrown in the can and shaken together with the old socialist screws. But no matter how hard the can was shaken, it remained the same old can with loose screws inside it. Like previous reforms, *perestroika* failed. Nobody wanted the can. Nobody wanted the screws.

*Lesson 4: Reforms of socialism should not be confused with the abandonment or replacement of socialism,*

*and*

*Lesson 5: The Western foreign economic policies produce different outcomes if applied to reforming socialist economies, economies that have abandoned socialism but not yet instituted a new system, and economies where socialism has been replaced with a new (capitalist) model.*

East European countries finally junked the old socialist tin can and decided to give it away. The problem, however, is that with no coherent new system of macro-economic management in place, much of the condemned socialist system continues in use. Rather than assisting in the building of the new economic institutional framework, the condemned socialist system frequently obstructs the process of transformation.

While the *economic structures* the West deals with when it trades with the East now are diversifying, *forms* of foreign economic relations remain the same. The main forms of foreign economic relations used in dealing with all three types of economic structures are foreign trade and capital investment flows from the West to take the form of joint ventures (JVs) or foreign direct investment (FDI). All of these are good acquaintances from the old days of East-West trade.[12] In these circumstances, one must be clear about the stages of transformation through which socialist economic structures pass. *Stage One* is the starting point of a socialist economic structure or a reforming socialist economic structure. In *Stage Two*, the condemned but still functioning socialist economic structure is retained, while a new, genuinely post-socialist economic structure is being built. Only in *Stage Three* do fully transformed economic structures appear.

Since the transformation from socialism has begun only recently, most East European countries are still far from Stage Three and do not have the new economic structure in place. When East Germany and West Germany unified economically and politically in 1990, East Germany was suddenly immersed in a Western economic and political structure. As the other Eastern European countries frequently pointed out, they did not have the East German option of merging with a Western state. Neither Hong Kong and Taiwan nor the Cuban exile community in the United States can be reasonably expected to perform the role of West Germany to China and Cuba respectively.[13]

Poland and Hungary, as East European countries that first embarked on a course of serious economic reforms in the 1970s, lead in the intensity of their foreign economic relations with the West.

Hungary, Poland, and the Czech Republic exhibit clear features of post-socialist economic structure. The fate of the other former CMEA, post-socialist countries is less clear. Both Bulgaria and Romania have declared only a tentative commitment to install new economic structures, and their socialist characteristics continue to be obvious.

There is a danger that countries presently at Stage Two may not make it and either will become stuck in a debilitating transition or slide back into Stage One. Since there is no realistic hope of returning to a functioning socialist structure, such prospects have frightening political implications.

The history of relations with the Soviet bloc furnishes ample examples of Western foreign economic relations with Stage One socialist economic structures. China, still maintaining the primary features of the Stalinist model of a centrally planned economy, provides an example of a bold foreign economic "open-door policy" advancing in the field of foreign economic relations further than some ex-socialist countries already at Stage Two.[14] Cuba's foreign economic initiatives fall also into this category.

## *Lesson 6: The role of foreign economic relations in influencing the collapse of socialism and assisting the post-socialist transition should not be overstated.*

The socialist country engaged in foreign economic relations with the West is typically anxious to preserve the integrity of its system and to avoid destabilizing side effects of these relations. The impetus for capitalist countries to enter these relations derives from the search for markets or geopolitical considerations (often overriding other concerns). There are two schools of thought in regard to the value of these engagements: 1) liberals believe that capitalist economic intervention will accelerate the demise of the socialist system, and 2) conservatives argue that capitalist economic intervention merely postpones the demise of the system.

The East European experience seems to confirm this latter conclusion. It is possible to show that foreign economic relations before the collapse of socialism made little or no difference to the economy, let alone to the timing of socialism's collapse. More surprisingly, even in the wake of the collapse of socialism, foreign economic relations continued to be relatively insignificant.

The evidence to date suggests that a successful transition to new economic structures is most dependent on the quality of domestic economic reform and not on the development of foreign economic relations. The success of foreign trade reforms, import liberalization, and introduction of currency convertibility ultimately depend on the progress achieved in the implementation of market-oriented reforms in the domestic economy as a whole, as well as on its macroeconomic development.

This is not to underestimate the importance of attempts to integrate with the world economy. As Nuti pointed out, foreign economic relations have a central role in the East European design of system replacement: they provide market signals, competition where there is monopoly, opportunities for reducing structural imbalances; they provide technology, management and capital, as well as more efficient ways of securing goods and services.[15] Most of the changes in foreign economic relations since the collapse of socialism, however, have been

> . . . largely ineffective because they have been incomplete and because they have preceded rather than followed a number of steps [in domestic reform] which were a precondition of reform success. Foreign trade reform has been the line of least resistance, i.e., the area in which changes have been easiest to formulate and implement. Changes in international institutions and policies can very often be done at the stroke of the pen: it is simple to devalue the currency, to enable a number of enterprises to trade whether or not they are ready to do it, to auction some foreign exchange. This is why there has been so much action on foreign economic relations, and so little effectiveness.[16]

Let us review the main forms of foreign economic relations as they developed in East-West relations and were applied before and after the collapse of socialism.

*Foreign trade, import and export,* was traditionally the only form of interaction with the West tolerated by the East. In these circumstances, with a country's economic relations confined to foreign trade and with imports and exports subjected to centralized control, the socialist economy was perceived to be insulated from outside interference. The central planner's concern was to determine the point beyond which an increased reliance on imports to balance domestic supply deficit might leave the centrally planned economy vulnerable to outside pressures. The fear of many planners was that relaxation of import policy could eventually threaten the very core values of the Soviet-style goal of creating an autarchic, self-sufficient industrial system.

Throughout the existence of the Soviet bloc, there was little danger of crossing this threshold. The obstacles to import-export trade, both self-imposed and imposed by the West, kept the volume of trade insignificant. In the post-socialist stage, most obstacles to foreign trade have been removed by the West and by the post-socialist countries that liberalized their trade policies, custom duties, and non-tariff commercial policy instruments and joined all international organizations facilitating trade. Among the first post-socialist measures in country after country has been the abolishment of the privileged monopoly position of the state appointed import-export agencies.

In the view of many western observers, it is through domestic economic reform and the improvement of product quality that the post-socialist countries will enhance their international economic standing. As Oppenheimer put it, upgrading of economic relations with western market economies should be oriented toward upgrading of products rather than of upgrading forms of cooperation. Some of these "higher forms of cooperation," regarded by the post-socialist countries as more desirable than simple liberalized trade, actually put the post-socialist countries at a disadvantage[17] by institutionalizing their backwardness and marginalizing them in the world economy.[18]

Among these "higher forms of economic cooperation," joint ventures and foreign direct investment are high on the agendas of all the post-socialist countries. The invention of JVs is associated with the Soviets' desperate attempts to liberalize in face of mounting economic problems. FDI was prohibited altogether until recently and thus continues to have the taste of forbidden fruit.

*Joint venture* is a more sophisticated form of cooperation than forms such as subcontracts or joint projects. JVs are, in fact, akin to combined licensing and subcontracting agreements.[19] One of the harbingers was a 1966 agreement by Fiat, the Italian automaker, to build a plant in the Soviet Union for the production of the *Dzhigule* car (which East Europeans often called the Fiatov). When East Europeans were allowed to follow the Soviet lead in the early 1970s, cooperation agreements between Western firms and East European enterprises became increasingly common. The East entered these JV agreements to acquire Western technology, improve competitiveness, and reduce foreign exchange needs. Western firms were motivated by the desire to gain access to Eastern markets and the opportunity to reduce production costs.[20]

If one discounts inflated claims of the propaganda leaflets published in the Soviet bloc advertising JVs, records of the number and performance of JVs before the implosion of socialism shows that they played a very insignificant role. For example, Hungary passed its law on foreign investment in 1972, but until the early 1980s, there were only three JVs. In 1988, there were 250 with 100 percent foreign participation (with the total volume of investments of $250 million). In 1989, there were 1,000 such enterprises ($300 million); in 1990, 3,600 ($900 million); in 1991, 5,500 ($1.4 billion). By May 1992, there were 12,000 joint ventures with a total foreign investment of $3.5 billion.[21] While the Hungarians forged forward, Czechoslovakia, still being punished for its 1968 "Prague Spring," was the last bloc state allowed to recognize JVs. Between 1948 and 1988, the Czechoslovak legal system lacked any structure for capital flows between the domestic economy and the outside world, and thus there was no flow. The first law on joint ventures, adopted in 1988, treated JVs as an oddity, exempting them from foreign exchange regulations and state subsidies but forcing them to be self-financing.

The JV legislation of all the CMEA countries had to be revised several times to provoke interest from the western firms. The first versions offered too-modest incentives and very severely restricted rights of the foreign joint venture partner in the host country. Only after revisions in the late 1980s did the incentives improve sufficiently to generate a change. Special preferences were finally offered concerning taxation and tariffs, labor relations, and investment. Despite these improved incentives, at the end of 1988 only $200 million was invested in Hungary, and there was a marked absence of significant multinational corporations among those investors.

The bloc countries changed their JV laws after the collapse of socialism, and most of them now allow majority, indeed 100 percent, western capital participation and control, with provisions for profit repatriation. The joint ventures, a form of foreign direct investment, become something of a misnomer with 100 percent western equity permitted. The expression JV (in English) is still used since the participation of a citizen of the post-socialist country is still required, in contrast to other forms of FDI. To the dismay of the post-socialist countries, the impact of JVs still continues to be very modest. This is partly due to investor uncertainty concerning political stability, access to domestic inputs, transferability, and liquidation of capital stakes.[22]

JVs became "a catchword for cheap, quick and efficient capital inflow" for leaders of bloc countries.[23] They failed to realize that western business people cannot be attracted simply by offering tax incentives: more important are infrastructural preconditions and the stability of the economic and legal order. According to a survey of 1,114 German firms, West German enterprises rated highest the facility offered by JVs of opening new markets and expected from these new foreign markets higher dynamics of sales. The features of the JV laws most advertised by the post-socialist countries were less attractive. Lower labor costs were ranked in sixth place, tax incentives in eighth, and subsidies for promoting incentives in the seventeenth place.[24]

JVs have not intensified the volume of trade, and their contribution to export production remains small since most of them are in consultancy and other services, rather than in manufacturing. As Oppenheimer puts it, "Most existing JVs in Poland are merely a form of arbitrage by former Polish residents."[25]

The story of successes from Spain, where about 50 percent of the manufacturing industry is based on FDI and JVs, confirms the thesis that the situation cannot be expected to change until (at least) the legal basis of the market economy has been firmly established. Required changes include establishment of the law of property (including land), contract law, company law, the existence of functioning financial institutions, and reasonable labor and tax laws. Foreign investors will require guaranteed convertibility of their financial stake; they require the right to repatriate both the locally earned profit and a portion of the value of capital assets.

The Chinese experience may prove of special interest to those considering investing in Cuba. Under the "open-door policy," JVs are now strongly encouraged as a form of cooperation with the West. In China, the safeguards for the western partner are regarded as sufficient: since neither party to the JV could continue production independently, there is no incentive for the host socialist country to expropriate the non-human, particularly knowledge-based, assets of the multi-national corporations. Other potential problems, such as upholding possible export restrictions, would be easier to deal with in a continuing relationship. An additional advantage is a low foreign exchange requirement, especially in case of a buy-back form of JV.[26]

Western investors regarded JVs as a temporary measure since potential foreign investors were interested in equity investment (minority or majority) and eventually also in portfolio investment. Countries wishing to adhere to socialism, however, saw FDI as dangerous because FDI exposed their economies to Western influences in a manner that could never be tolerated. In the Soviet model for a centrally planned economy, the international mobility of capital is anathema. As this ideological and theoretical roadblock became apparent to potential investors, investment dried up. Foreign capital was attracted to the Soviet economy for the last time during the 1920s, beyond which point, until new legislation in 1987, for ideological and other reasons it was stopped.[27]

Today even socialist countries have revised their view of FDI. China's open-door policy bears this out: FDI directly helps to relieve domestic capital supply bottlenecks and to promote employment and economic growth. By contrast, increased capital formation through imports of machinery and equipment must be financed by extra export earnings.[28] The danger for China continues to be the erosion of socialist planning: for example, to the extent that FDI promotes import substitution (to substitute for direct imports production for the domestic market), the primacy of central planning may have to give way to accommodation of foreign interests. This is inherently subversive to the entire system of central planning. FDI may also undermine another pillar of socialist economy structures, the system of foreign exchange control.

The fixation in East Europe on attracting FDI derives from the fact that because of the high external indebtedness of most East European countries except Romania, many Eastern European economists feel that direct investment will be the only accessible source of foreign capital into the indefinite future.[29]

Despite the growing attractiveness of FDI, obstacles remain on both Western and Eastern sides. East Europeans report institutional and psychological concerns. There is a feeling among some Eastern

Europeans that until domestic reform is completed, competitive domestic capital funds emerge, problems of lack of experienced personnel and shortage of convertible currencies are resolved, and domestic currency distortions are corrected, there is the risk of national property being sold off on unfavorable terms. It is argued that FDI, therefore, should not take off until privatization is well under way and domestic capital formation is significantly enlarged. Even in Hungary, in the most liberal of East European countries, it is feared that since an unprecedentedly high proportion of the national assets are to be sold in an economy that still lacks functioning capital market and sizeable domestic demand for capital goods, both FDI and privatization will be harmful.[30] Furthermore, it is argued, the valuation of ailing state assets is uncertain because of earlier distorted accounting practices, inflation, and the lack of capital markets and operational linkages with international capital markets.

Concern in the West focuses on the incompleteness of domestic economic reform. It is argued that western entrepreneurs will opt for direct investment rather than direct trade only if the cost of direct exchange is too high (of monitoring quality, the delivery date, and so on) or if the entrepreneur can capture a monopoly position, at present an unlikely situation.

In favor of foreign economic relations, economists on both sides agree that FDI and JVs can increase economic activities, play a major role in easing the foreign exchange constraints on domestic expenditure, bring much needed organizational skills and quality control, and ease entry to western markets.[31] So far, however, the expectations have not been fulfilled.

The most powerful argument against rushing foreign economic relations returns the debate to the question of domestic economic reform: as soon as Eastern Europe reaches the mean OECD level of development, capital networks will emerge almost automatically.[32] In this view, foreign investment now is at best wasteful, at worst, counterproductive.[33]

## Lesson 7: Based on the historical record, the collapse of Soviet-style socialism where it still endures should be anticipated, but the timing and form of that collapse is not predictable.

The only certainty is that the post-socialist transformation will be extremely difficult and painful. Economists and political scientists agree that there is no general theory of transformation of centrally planned economies into market economies.[34] In each country, the level of economic development, the degree of integration into the international economy, the imbalances of supply and demand differ; also, the degree of shortages, the infrastructure, the information network, the communications system, and the mentality and education level of the populations differ.[35] What the East Europeans share is the experience of declining domestic production levels, rising unemployment, falling real wages and living standards, and deteriorating internal and external economic balances.

In East Europe no advance will be made until privatization gets off the ground. The difficulties are enormous: state-owned enterprises are based on out-of-date technology, capital equipment is run down, and there is no demand for the products of the enterprises in the markets, especially the western markets at which all East Europeans aim. Many of the enterprises have been closed because of their catastrophic effects on the environment. Production units are inefficient. The introduction of real money while prices remain under control makes little sense. Reform of the external trade regimes and progress toward convertibility of the currency are part and parcel of the construction of a market system internally and should proceed in parallel with it.[36]

The most tragic aspect of the story of the transformation is that once East Europe is "transformed," per capita income levels are likely to be in the same range as Middle Eastern and Asian countries, well below those of Western Europe. The Czechs, for example, realize that had they not had the misfortune of becoming incorporated into CMEA they would now have been on par with Singapore. Bulgaria would have a per capita GNP similar to South Korea. Instead, Bulgaria is at the level of Mexico and Czechoslovakia at the level of Greece. Hungary and Poland are at the level of Argentina. Average per capita income in 1990 would place the Soviet Union also roughly at the level of Argentina.[37] This means that when the post-socialist transformation is completed, East European countries will have reached the level of developing countries, not the levels of the developed West. It can be expected that after the first transition the levels may drop even further, because so much embodied capital, both physical and intellectual, is ill-adapted or obsolete and will have to be discarded before true growth can begin. Then comes the second transition, from developing to developed. This second transition will be long and arduous even if the first transition is successful. The damage caused by socialism is indeed profound and in some cases may be irreversible.

## *Lessons for Investors in Cuba*

What then, are the lessons from the rest of the socialist world for those considering investment in Cuba, either today, under the moribund Castro regime, or in the future, when Cuban socialism is replaced by some sort of post-socialist economy? I pretend to no expertise on Cuba, but if the experience of East Europe as summarized in this paper is a guide, two tentative points are worth consideration.

Socialism as an economic system stopped functioning some time ago. The final implosion of socialism in any given country, like its installation, is a political act. Before the political implosion, other than adding to political pressure, Western economic intervention is wasteful and ineffective. Journalists, political scientists, and politicians might recommend investment in Cuba now, but no sensible capitalist would choose Cuba as a site for investment.

After the implosion, the issue of investment in Cuba will be a matter for discussion by academics and politicians, in much the same way as the debate over the current U.S. trade embargo against Cuba is conducted on political, not economic, grounds. However, no matter what form that discussion takes, capital will not flow in significant volume into Cuba so long as conditions remain inclement. For those who wish a post-socialist Cuba well, the lesson of East Europe is that in the aftermath of the implosion, assistance to Cuba should be economic but should emphasize rebuilding domestic economic structures in the shortest possible time. If they draw on the accumulating East European experience, Cubans need not repeat the East European mistakes. But unless they, and those who would assist them, pay attention to East Europe's experience, they will.

# NOTES

[1] I would like to thank Dr. Henry Hamman for his linguistic assistance with the preparation of this paper.

[2] Domenico Mario Nuti, "Socialism on Earth," Inaugural lecture, unpublished paper, University of Birmingham, April 28, 1981.

[3] Nuti, "Socialism on Earth." The discussion of models of socialism also draws on P.J.D. Wiles, 1962, *The Political Economy of Communism* (London and New York: Oxford University Press).

[4] Peter Wiles, ed., 1982, *The New Communist Third World: An Essay in Political Economy* (London and Canberra: Croom Helm) 13ff, quoted and developed in V. Kubalkova and A. A. Cruickshank, 1989, *Marxism and International Relations* (Oxford and New York: Oxford University Press) 117ff.

[5] The USSR attended the Bretton Woods Conference but refused to sign the resulting agreements or join the International Monetary Fund (IMF) and the International Bank for Reconstruction and Development (IBRD). Czechoslovakia and Poland, which initially joined the fund and the bank, withdrew in 1950 and 1954, respectively, under strong Soviet pressure. East European countries were not allowed to accept Marshall Plan aid or to accede to the General Agreement on Tariffs and Trade (GATT). See Joan E. Spero, 1990, *The Politics of International Economic Relations,* fourth edition (New York: St. Martin's Press) 307.

[6] In 1938, 10 percent of eastern exports went to eastern countries (including the Soviet Union), 68 percent to Western Europe, 4 percent to the United States and Canada, and 5 percent to Latin America. By 1953, 64 percent of eastern exports went to eastern countries, 14 percent to Western Europe, and less than 1 percent to the United States, Canada, and Latin America. The balance of Eastern European trade was with other areas of the world such as Asia and Africa (Spero, 1990, *The Politics of International Economic Relations*).

[7] Spero, 1990, *The Politics of International Economic Relations,* 309.

[8] U.S. Department of State, 1974, *The Battle Act Report 1973, Mutual Defense Assistance Control Act of 1951, Twenty-Sixth Report to Congress* (Washington, D.C.: U.S. Government Printing Office) 22.

[9] U.S. Department of State, 1974, *The Battle Act Report 1973,* 18.

[10] O. Lange, 1967, "The Computer and the Market," in *Capitalism, Socialism and Economic Growth — Essays in Honour of Maurice Dobb,* ed. C.H. Feinstein (Cambridge: Cambridge University Press).

[11] Quoted in Spero 1990, 312. See also Bohumil Urban, 1990, "Transformace ekonomik postko munistickych zemi a odpovednost demokratickeho spolecenstvi Evropy," (Transformation of the economies of the post-communist countries and the responsibility of the democratic commonwealth of Europe), unpublished paper, 1990.

[12] Hans-Jurgen Wagener, 1991, "Economic Relations with Market Economies: A Discussion," in *Reforms in Foreign Economic Relations of Eastern Europe and the Soviet Union,* eds. Michael Kaiser and Aleksandar Vacic, Economic Studies No. 2 (New York: United Nations Economic Commission for Europe) 116.

[13] For the volume of foreign investment in China, see Y.Y. Kueh, 1992, "Foreign Investment and Economic Change in China," *The China Quarterly* No. 131, September.

[14] Kueh 1992, 638.

[15] D.M. Nuti, "Progress in Trade Reforms, Missing Links, Convertibility: A Discussion," in Kaiser and Vacic 1991, 49.

[16] Nuti in Kaiser and Vacic 1991.

[17] Peter Oppenheimer, "Economic Reforms and Traditional Policies: Summary of Discussion," in Kaiser and Vacic 1991, 61.

[18] For discussion of the concept of the new international division of labor (NIDL), see F. Frobel et al., 1980, *The New International Division of Labor: Structural Unemployment in Industrialized Countries and Industrialization in Developing Countries* (Cambridge: Cambridge University Press).

[19] *Developing the East European Market,* 1966, (Geneva: Business Europe) 58.

[20] There is a considerable literature about JVs. See, for example, *East-West Joint Venture Contracts,* 1989, Volume 1 of the *Guide on Legal Aspects of New Forms of Industrial Cooperation* (New York: Economic Commission for Europe, United Nations). Yuri Nechaev and Natalia Ogarkova, 1991, "Joint Ventures: Inside Glance," *Foreign Trade* no. 9 (Moscow). Tatiana Cheklina, 1991, "Joint Ventures in Eastern Europe," *Foreign Trade* no. 8 (Moscow). Tatyana Artemova, 1989, "Joint Ventures: Progress and Prospects," *Foreign Trade* no. 7 (Moscow). Sergei Manezhev, 1988, "Foreign Investment in the Socialist Economy," *Foreign Trade* no. 12 (Moscow). Lyudmila Rodina, 1988, "Socialist-Capitalist Joint Ventures," *Foreign Trade* no. 10 (Moscow). Vadim Teperman, 1988, "Joint Enterprise in Hungary," *Foreign Trade* no. 7 (Moscow). Vladimir Kravchenko and Edgar Pleskanovsky, 1988, "The People's Republic of China: Joint Ventures with Foreign Participation," *Foreign Trade* no. 2 (Moscow). Pavel Smirnov, 1988, "Joint Ventures on Soviet Territory (first agreements and the development of legal regulation)," *Foreign Trade* no. 1 (Moscow). Vyacheslav Kormyshev and Sergei Ryabikov, 1987, "Legal Aspects

of the Establishment and Operation in Socialist Countries of Joint Ventures in which Capitalist Firms Participate," *Foreign Trade* no. 11 (Moscow). Andrzej Tynel, 1987, "Poland: the Law on Joint-Stock Companies in which Foreign Capital Participates," *Foreign Trade* no. 5 (Moscow). Philip Hanson, 1991, "Joint Ventures Still Expanding despite Everything," *Report on the USSR* (Munich: Radio Free Europe/Radio Liberty — RFE/RL) August 9 (3): 32. Saulius Girnius, 1991, "Foreign Investment in Lithuania," *Report on the USSR* (Munich: RFE/RL) August 2 (3): 31. Patrice Dabrowski, 1991, "The Foreign Investment Boom," *Report on Eastern Europe* (Munich: RFE/RL) July 26 (2): 30. Paul Gafton, 1990, "New Provisions for Foreign Investment in Romania," *Report on Eastern Europe* (Munich: RFE/RL) June 15 (1): 24. Roman Stefanowski, 1990, "Efforts to Increase the Attraction of Joint Ventures," *Report on Eastern Europe* (Munich: RFE/RL) April 13 (1): 15. Paul Marer and Wlodzimierz Siwinski, eds., 1988, *Creditworthiness and Reform in Poland* (Bloomington: Indiana University Press). Jozef M. van Brabant, ed., 1989, *Economic Integration in Eastern Europe: A Handbook* (New York: Routledge, New York). Martin Schnitzer, 1980, *U.S. Business Involvement in Eastern Europe: Case Studies of Hungary, Poland and Romania* (New York: Praeger). Marie Lavigne, ed., 1990, *The Soviet Union and Eastern Europe in the Global Economy* (London, New York: Cambridge University Press). Alan B. Sherr, Ivan S. Korolev, Igor P. Faminsky, Tatyana M. Artemova, and E.L. Yakovleva, eds., 1991, *International Joint Ventures: Soviet and Western Perspectives* (New York, Westport, London: Quorum Books). C.T. Saunders, ed., 1977, *East-West Cooperation in Business: Inter-firm Studies* (Vienna, New York: Springer-Verlag). Jozef M. van Brabant, ed., 1993, *The New Eastern Europe and the World Economy* (Boulder, Oxford: Westview Press). Paul Marer and John Michael Montias, eds., 1980, *East European Integration and East-West Trade* (Bloomington: Indiana University Press).

[21] Viktor Durnev, 1993, "The Practice of Attracting Foreign Capital to East European Countries," *Foreign Trade* no. 1 (Moscow) 24.

[22] Nuti in Kaiser and Vacic 1991, 50.

[23] Horst Brezinski in Kaiser and Vacic 1991, 47.

[24] Brezinski in Kaiser and Vacic 1991, 47.

[25] Oppenheimer in Kaiser and Vacic 1991, 61.

[26] Raissa Chan and Michael Hoy, 1991, "East-West Joint Ventures and Buyback Contracts," *Journal of International Economics* 30, 341-342.

[27] Bykov in Kaiser and Vacic 1991, 41.

[28] Kueh 1992, 637.

[29] The debt figures are misleading. Most East European countries have an "internal debt," obsolete capital stock, accumulated need of investment for ecological protection, and a lack of up-to-date infrastructure.

[30] Miroslav Hmcir in Kaiser and Vacic 1991, 12.

[31] Oppenheimer in Kaiser and Vacic 1991, 61.

[32] Wagener in Kaiser and Vacic 1991, 116.

[33] The Polish strategy during 1961-1983 of increasing efficiency through western capital imports appears to have been misguided, since the marginal product of western capital was lower than that of domestic capital already during the 1960s. Importations of western capital, in fact, exacerbated these differentials. See Katherine Terrell, 1992, "Productivity of Western and Domestic Capital in Polish Industry," *Journal of Comparative Economics* 16.

[34] Sarah Meiklejohn Terry, 1993, "Thinking About Post-Communist Transitions: How Different Are They?" *Slavic Review* 52: (2, Summer) 333-338.

[35] Peter Murrell, 1990, "Big Bangs versus Evolution: East European Economic Reforms in the Light of Recent Economic History," *PlanEcon* 6: (26, June) 1.

[36] Oppenheimer in Kaiser and Vacic 1991, 59.

[37] Jean Baneth in Kaiser and Vacic 1991, 57 ff.

*Appendix I*

# CUBAN FOREIGN INVESTMENT LAWS

# GACETA OFICIAL

## DE LA REPUBLICA DE CUBA

EXTRAORDINARIA   LA HABANA, LUNES 15 DE FEBRERO DE 1982   AÑO LXXX

Imprenta: Zanja No. 352, esq. a Escobar. - Habana 2

Número 3                                                   Página 11

## CONSEJO DE ESTADO

FIDEL CASTRO RUZ, Presidente del Consejo de Estado
de la República de Cuba.

HAGO SABER: Que el Consejo de Estado ha aprobado
lo siguiente:

POR CUANTO: El desarrollo económico nacional ha permitido
en los últimos años la realización de actividades lucrativas en asociación
con intereses extranjeros en distintos países, las cuales se han
formalizado mediante la constitución de empresas mixtas de capital
cubano y foráneo y a través de otras formas de asociación económica
bilateral y multilateral.

POR CUANTO: En los últimos años también se ha dado inicio a
determinadas formas de asociación económica con intereses extranjeros
dentro del territorio nacional, sin que hayan estado reguladas de
manera específica en la legislación.

POR CUANTO: Estas asociaciones, promovidas, o aceptadas de
forma absolutamente libre por el Estado Socialista, ayudan a la
consolidación de nuestro sistema económico y social.

POR CUANTO: Conviene establecer un régimen jurídico bajo el
cual puedan continuar desarrollándose en el territorio nacional las
asociaciones económicas de empresas estatales cubanas y otros entes
nacionales con entidades extranjeras, dentro de los lineamientos de la
política vigente en este aspecto de las relaciones económicas

internacionales, que tiene entre sus objetivos esenciales la expansión de las exportatciones y del turísmo extranjero.

POR TANTO: El consejo de Estado, en ejercicio de la atribución que le está conferida por el inciso c) del artículo 88 de la Constitución de la República, acuerda dictar el siguiente.

## DECRETO-LEY NUMERO 50
## SOBRE ASOCIACION ECONOMICA ENTRE ENTIDADES CUBANAS Y EXTRANJERAS

### CAPITULO I
### REGIMEN JURIDICO

ARTICULO 1.- El Comité Ejecutivo del Consejo de Ministros designará una comisión facultada para autorizar que empresas estatales y otras organizaciones nacionales se unan en asociación económica con intereses extranjeros, dentro del territorio nacional para llevar a cabo actividades lucrativas que coadyuven al desarrollo del país.

Las asociaciones económicas a que se refiere el párrafo anterior pueden adoptar la forma de empresas mixtas de capital cubano y extranjero, con personalidad y patrimonio propios, u otras formas diversas que no signifiquen la creación de una persona jurídica.

La comisión a que se refiere el primer párrafo de este artículo se designa en lo adelante como "la Comisión".

ARTICULO 2.- El Comité Ejecutivo del Consejo de Ministros puede facultar a la Comisión para autorizar que empresas estatales u otras organizaciones nacionales arrienden a empresas mixtas de las que se mencionan en el Artículo anterior, o aporten a las mismas en usufructo temporal, como capital, terrenos o instalaciones industriales, turísticas o de otro tipo, existentes o que se construyan en el territorio nacional.

ARTICULO 3.- Al otorgar cada autorización la Comisión establece las condiciones a que deberán someterse las asociaciones económicas, así como los arrendamientos y los aportes en usufructo temporal a empresas mixtas.

No son aplicables a los arrendamientos mencionados en el párrafo anterior las disposiciones legales vigentes sobre arrendamiento de bienes.

ARTICULO 4.- El término de duración que se fije para las asociaciones económicas debe propiciar la recuperación del capital invertido y la obtención de ganancias que hagan atractiva dicha inversión para ambas partes.

ARTICULO 5.- En las asociaciones económicas que se constituyen en el país participan:

Por Cuba: las empresas y uniones de empresas estatales y otras organizaciones nacionales.

Por la parte extranjera: las empresas y otras entidades económicas establecidas en el exterior, estatales o privadas, dedicadas a actividades lucrativas, cualquiera que sea su forma jurídica, incluyendo la persona natural.

ARTICULO 6.- Las empresas mixtas que se constituyen al amparo de lo dispuesto en el presente Decreto-Ley adoptan la forma de compañias anónimas por acciones nominativas, y a ellas les son de aplicación las disposiciones del Código de Comercio vigente.

ARTICULO 7.- Las empresas mixtas tienen nacionalidad cubana y su domicilio en el territorio nacional. Pueden crear oficinas, representaciones, sucursales y filiales en el extrnajero, así como tener participaciones en entidades en el exterior.

ARTICULO 8.- El funcionamiento de las empresas mixtas y las relaciones entre los socios se regulan por el convenio de asociación y los estatutos orgánicos que se suscríban.

El convenio de asociación contiene los pactos fundamentales entre los socios para la conducción y el desarrollo de las operaciones de la empresa mixta, así como para la consecución de sus objetivos, entre ellos los que garantizan la administración o la coadministración de la empresa por la parte cubana y los relativos al mercado que cada parte asegura para la producción o los servicios de la empresa.

Los estatutos orgánicos de la empresa mixta incluyen disposiciones relacionadas con la oraganización y operación de la entidad, entre ellas las referidas a la junta de accionistas, sus atribuciones y organización; el quórum requerido y los requisitos que se exijan para el ejercicio del derecho de voto en la junta de accionistas; la estructura y las atribuciones de la junta de directores; el método mediante el cual estas entidades adoptan sus decisionnes, tanto en la junta de accionistas como en la junta de directores, el cual puede ser desde la simple mayoría hasta la unanimidad; el nombramiento, atribuciones, remuneración y responsabilidad de los funcionarios de la gerencia de la empresa; las bases del sitema de contabilidad; el cálculo y distribución de las utilidades; el método para liquidar activos fijos; los casos de disolución y el procedimiento para liquidar la empresa; así como otras estipulaciones que resulten del presente Decreto-Ley y del acuerdo de las partes.

ARTICULO 9.- Las formas restantes de asociación económica se instrumentan mediante contratos de asociación.

El contenido de los contratos de asociación se acuerda entre las partes en función del objetivo de la asociación.

ARTICULO 10.- Las empresas mixtas adquieren personalidad jurídica, y los contratos a que se refiere el Artículo 9 entran en vigor, cuando son inscriptos en el registro que sobre tales actividades organiza y regula la Cámara de Comercio de la República de Cuba, sin que a ese fin se requiera ninguna otra inscripción.

ARTICULO 11.- Creada una empresa mixta, u otorgado un contrato de asociación económica, no pueden cambiar los partícipes sino por acuerdo unánime de las partes.

ARTICULO 12.- Las empresas mixtas se modifican, disuelven y liquidan conforme a sus disposiciones estatutarias, y las demás formas de asociación económica con arreglo al contrato de asociación. En ambos casos se aplica el Código de Comercio de manera supletoria.

Las modificaciones y disoluciones se inscriben en el registro de la Cámara de Comercio al cual se refiere el Artículo 10.

ARTICULO 13.- Los conflictos que surjan de las relaciones entre las partes de una empresa mixta se resuelven según lo acordado en los convenios de asociación y en los estatutos orgánicos de la empresa.

Los conflictos entre los socios de otras formas de asociación económica se ventilan según lo que establece el contrato de asociación.

## CAPITULO II
## REGULACIONES FINANCIERAS

ARTICULO 14.- El capital de la empresa mixta, y las aportaciones de las partes en el caso de otras formas de asociación económica pueden estar constituidos por efectivo y demás bienes, incluyendo el usufructo temporal de terrenos y otros inmuebles; materias primas, materiales, herramientas y cualquier otro activo.

Los aportes de capital a una empresa mixta, y las aportaciones de las partes en las demás formas de asociación económica en los casos procedentes, se cuantifican en la moneda libremente convertible y sobre las bases de valoración que se convengan por sus partícipes.

ARTICULO 15.- La participación extranjera en el capital de la empresa mixta tiene el límite del 49%, salvo en los casos excepcionales en que el Comité Ejecutivo del Consejo de Ministros autorice una participación mayor.

ARTICULO 16.- La Comisión, antes de autorizar la creación de la empresa mixta o el establecimienito de otra forma de asociación económica, puede exigir al posible socio extranjero que preste una garantía adecuada de que realizará su aportación.

Si la garantía es prestada en efectivo, devenga los intereses del mercado.

ARTICULO 17.- Prestada una garantía con arreglo a lo señalado en el Artículo anterior, la misma queda liberada:

a) si la Comisión autoriza la creación de la empresa mixta o el establecimiento de otra forma de asociación económica. En este caso la garantía, si fuese en efectivo, se transfiere con sus intereses a la asociación como parte de la aportación del socio extranjero. Si la garantía fuese en valores, se devuelve al depositante;

b) si la Comisión deniega la solicitud o si no se pronuncia sobre ella en un plazo de 60 días. En estos casos la garantía, y sus intereses cuando proceda, quedan a la libre disposición del que la prestó.

ARTICULO 18.- Las empresas mixtas arrendatarias o usufructarias de instalaciones industriales, turísticas o de cualquier tipo, aseguran dichas instalaciones a favor del arrendador cubano o del que hace el aporte.

Las empresas de seguros cubanas tienen el derecho de primera opción en la venta de las pólizas, sobre la base de primas y demás condiciones contractuales competitivas a escala internacional.

ARTICULO 19.- Las empresas mixtas, y las partes de las otras formas de asociación económica en los casos procedentes, abren cuentas en moneda libremente convertible en un banco del sistema bancario nacional, a través de las cuales efectúan los cobros y pagos que generan sus operaciones.

ARCTICULO 20.- Se aplican las tasas de cambio oficiales del Banco Nacional de Cuba para:

a) la valoración en moneda libremente convertible de servicios, salarios y otras prestaciones cuando se cobran sobre la base de tarifas expresadas en moneda nacional;

b) la conversión de los impuestos y otras obligaciones fiscales cuyo importe se expresa en moneda nacional;

c) cualquier otro canje de moneda.

ARTICULO 21.- Las empresas mixtas, y las partes en las demás formas de asociación económica, pueden concertar préstamos en moneda extranjera:

a) con un banco del sistema bancario nacional;

b) con bancos en el exterior, con arreglo a las regulaciones del Banco Nacional de Cuba sobre esta materia.

ARTICULO 22.- Las empresas mixtas, y las partes en las demás formas de asociación económica en los casos procedentes, constituyen, con cargo a sus utilidades, una reserva para cubrir las contingencias que pudieran producirse en sus operaciones, dentro de los límites y con arreglo a las regulaciones que establece el Comité Estatal de Finanzas.

ARTICULO 23.- El Estado cubano garantiza al socio extranjero la libre transferencia al exterior, en moneda libremente convertible, a través del Banco Nacional de Cuba, de los dividendos o utilidades netas que obtenga; del pago que reciba de la parte cubana en caso de que acuerde transferir a ésta toda o parte de su aportación, así como la parte que le corresponda de la liquidación de la asociación económica.

ARTICULO 24.- El Banco Nacional de Cuba puede dar garantía al socio extranjero de que, en caso de suspensión de actividades de la asociación económica por actos unilaterales del Estado cubano, podrá repatriar la parte que le corresponda de la liquidación de dicha asociación.

## CAPITUILO III
## OBLIGACIONES FISCALES

ARTICULO 25.- Las empresas mixtas, sus socios, dirigentes y funcionarios; así como las partes, sus dirigentes y funcionarios en las demás formas de asociación económica, están exentos del pago de los siguientes impuestos de los que establece la Ley 998, de 10 de enero de 1962:

a) sobre ingresos brutos percibidos por empresas privadas;

b) sobre ingresos personales;

c) sobre trasmisión de bienes immuebles y establecimientos mercantiles.

ARTICULO 26.- Las empresas mixtas y las partes en otras formas de asociación económica en los casos procedentes, son sujetos de los siguientes impuestos:

a) Sobre utilidades. El tipo impositivo es del 30% sobre la utilitdad neta anual. Será deducible de la utilidad neta imponible la parte de las utilidades que se reinvierta incrementando el capital social de la empresa mixta o las aportaciones a otro tipo de asociación económica; la que se destine a los fondos de estimulación económica de los trabajadores, así como la que se reserva para cubrir contingencias o con otros objetivos que acuerden las partes. Este impuesto se determina por años naturales y se paga dentro de los dos primeros meses del año siguiente.

b) Sobre ingresos de los trabajadores (Impuesto sobre Nóminas). El tipo impositívo es del 25% sobre la totalidad de los salarios y demás ingresos que por cualquier concepto perciban los trabajadores cubanos, excepto lo que reciban con cargo al fondo de estimulación económica de los trabajadores. En este impuesto queda incluida la contribución a la Seguridad Social. Se paga conjuntamente con los salarios y demás retribuciones del personal cubano.

c) Aranceles y demás derechos recaudables en las aduanas.

d) Sobre la propiedad o posesión de vehículos automotores de transporte terrestre.

e) Sobre documentos (tasas y derechos por la solicitud obtención o renovación de determinados documentos).

ARTICULO 27.- El pago de impuestos, aranceles y derechos se

realiza en moneda convertible, aun en aquellos casos en que su importe se expresa en moneda nacional.

ARTICULO 28.- El Comité Estatal de Finanzas, teniendo en cuenta los beneficios que la asociación pueda reportar a la economía nacional está facultado para eximir temporalmente a las empresas mixtas o a las partes de las demás formas de asociación económica, total o parcialmente, del impuesto sobre utilidades y de los aranceles y demás derechos recaudables en las aduanas.

ARTICULO 29.- Las empresas mixtas, y las partes de las demás formas de asociación económica en los casos procedentes, presentan al Comité Estatal de Finanzas en el término y las condiciones que éste establezca, los estados financieros que se les exijan, sin perjuicio de las auditorias oficiales que disponga dicho Comité Estatal.

ARTICULO 30.- Las partes asociadas pueden determinar librement el sistema de contabilidad más conveniente a los fínes de la asociación económica, siempre que el sistema adoptado se ajuste a los principios que universalmente se aceptan en este campo y que permita satisfacer las exigencias fiscales.

## CAPITULO IV
## REGULACIONES MERCANTILES

ARTICULO 31.- Las empresas mixtas, y las partes de las demás formas de asociación económica, tienen derecho a exportar su producción directamente, y a importar, también directamente, lo necesario para su fines.

ARTICULO 32.- Sin perjucio de lo dispuesto en el artículo anterior, las empresas estatales cubanas tienen el derecho de primera opción en cuanto a las siguientes operaciones, sobre la base de que ofrezcan a la empresa mixta o a las partes de las demás formas de asociación económica en los casos procedentes, precios y demás condiciones competitivas a escala internacional.

a)  suministro de combustible, materias primas, materiales, herramientas, equipos, piezas de repuesto, accesorios y bienes de consumo;

b) compra de la producción terminada o del servicio que preste la asociación económica;

c) transporte y seguro marítimos.

ARTICULO 33.- Las empresas mixtas, y las partes de las demás formas de asociación económica en los casos procendentes, tienen a su vez el derecho de primera opción para que las empresas estatales cubanas les compren los artículos que las asociaciones económicas sean capaces de producir en Cuba en sustitución de importaciones que dichas empresas estatales prevean hacer de países con los cuales Cuba no tenga suscrito convenio de pagos sobre la base de precios y demás condiciones competitivas a escala internacional.

ARTICULO 34.- Las empresas estatales cubanas garantizan a las empresas mixtas y a las partes de las demás formas de asociación económica en los casos procedentes, mediante contrato:

a) los suministros y servicios que acuerden con arreglo a los señalado en el Artículo 32;

b) el suministro de energía eléctrica, gas y agua; el servicio de teléfonos y teletipos locales e internacionales; el transporte nacional y los demás servicios no obtenibles por vía del comercio exterior.

ARTICULO 35.- Las empresas mixtas, y las partes de las demás formas de asociación económica son sujetos de los contratos económicos definidos en el Decreto-Ley No. 15, del 3 de julio de 1978, cuya concertación y ejecución se rigen por la legislación económica vigente.

Los conflictos entre las empresas mixtas y las partes de las demás formas de asociación económica con las empresas estatales y otras organizaciones nacionales respecto a la concertación o ejecución de contratos económicos se someten al Arbitraje Estatal.

## CAPITULO V
## REGIMEN LABORAL

ARTICULO 36.- La fuerza de trabajo que preste servicio en las empresas mixtas debe ser cubana, salvo la que las partes acuerden para cubrir determinados cargos de dirección o algunos puestos de trabajo de carácter técnico de alta especialización.

ARTICULO 37.- La entidad cubana que participa en la empresa mixta, u otra empresa o entidad cubana, contrata con la empresa mixta la utilización de la fuerza de trabajo cubana que ambas partes acuerdan, mediante el pago de una suma mensual equivalente al importe total de los salarios y demás remuneraciones devengados por el personal cubano.

ARTICULO 38.- Los trabajadores cubanos que prestan servicio a la empresa mixta, cualquiera que sea su categoría ocupacional, mantienen su relación contractual de trabajo con la entidad cubana que contrata la fuerza a dicha empresa.

La entidad cubana paga a dichos trabajadores sus salarios y demás remuneraciones.

ARTICULO 39.- Las empresas mixtas están obligadas a cumplir la legislación vigente sobre protección e higiene del trabajo.

ARTICULO 40.- La entidad cubana que contrata la fuerza de trabajo a la empresa mixta asume por su cuenta el pago de los salarios y demás derechos y prestaciones correspondientes a los trabajadores cubanos que por cualquier motivo cesen en la prestación de servicios a la empresa mixta, incluidas las indemnizaciones que en su caso dispongan las autoridades competentes.

ARTICULO 41.- Las tarifas salariales que cobra el personal cubano son las expresadas en la legislación vigente, salvo el caso del personal dirigente cubano, cuyos salarios son convenidos entre las partes de la asociación económica en correspondencia con el salario asignado al personal dirigente extranjero.

ARTICULO 42.- En las empresas mixtas es obligatoria la constitutción de un fondo de estimulación económica a los trabajadores cubanos. La cuantía de los aportes anuales a este fondo, su destino y operación son determinados conforme a las condiciones que dicta la Comisión al autorizar la creación de la empresa mixta.

ARTICULO 43.- La empresa mixta y las partes de las demás formas de asociación económica pueden contratar libremente al personal técnico y de administración extranjero que requieran, el que está sujeto a las leyes de inmigración y extranjería vigentes en Cuba. Los derechos y obligaciones de los trabajadores extranjeros se fijan por acuerdo de las partes.

ARTICULO 44.- Los trabajadores extranjeros pueden remesar al exterior el por ciento de sus salarios en divisas convertibles que determina el Banco Nacional de Cuba.

## DISPOSICIONES ESPECIALES

PRIMERA: Respecto a las zonas de alta significación para el turismo internacional, que autoriza la Ley de Protección del Medio Abiente y el Uso Racional de los Recursos Naturales (Ley No. 33 de 10 de enero de 1981) se autoriza:

a) al Comité Estatal de Finanzas, a declarar toda o parte de la zona libre de impuestos, aranceles de aduana, derechos, tasas y contribuciones;

b) al Comité Estatal de Trabajo y Seguridad Social a establecer un régimen laboral especial;

c) al Ministerio del Interior, a establecer un régimen especial de control de orden público y facilitar los trámites de inmigración a través del Instituto Nacional de Turismo.

SEGUNDA: Se faculta al Comité Ejecutivo del Consejo de Ministros para autorizar que empresas estatales u otras organizaciones nacionales arrienden a entidades extranjeras las instalaciones a que se refiere el Artículo 2 de este Decreto-Ley.

En este caso el arrendatario asegura lo que es objeto del arrendamiento a favor del arrendador.

El régimen laboral en las instalaciones arrendadas a entidades extranjeras es el que resulta del Capítulo V de este Decreto-Ley, con la salvedad de que en este caso la fuerza de trabajo cubana es contratada por la entidad arrendadora ó por otra empresa o entidad cubana, según decida el Comité Ejecutivo del Consejo de Ministros.

El Comité Ejecutivo del Consejo de oMinsitros dispone las demás condiciones del arrendamiento al otorgar cada autorización.

No se aplican a estos arrendamientos las disposiciones legales vigentes sobre arrendamiento de bienes.

TERCERA: Las empresas mixtas, la parte extranjera de otras formas de asociación económica y los arrendatarios extranjeros no están obligados a la observancia de lo dispuesto en la legislación relativa a la información clasificada.

CUARTA: Las disposiciones del presente Decreto-Ley no rigen para los acuerdos internacionales de compensación en los que participan las empresas estatales cubanas, los cuales se regulan:

a) por el Comité Estatal de Colaboración Económica, cuando

tienen como objeto la compra-venta de plantas completas, líneas de producción y otros objetivos industriales con financiamiento a largo o mediano plazo;

b) por el Ministerio del Comercio Exsterior, en los restantes casos.

QUINTA: Las estipulaciones del presente Decreto-Ley no rigen para la constitución de asociaciones económicas que se organicen en Cuba por acuerdo del Consejo de Ayuda Mutua Económica o del Sistema Económico Latinoamericano, o por acuerdo bilateral con un país miembro del CAME.

## DISPOSICION FINAL

UNICA: Se derogan cuantas disposiciones legales y reglamentarias se opongan a lo establecido en este Decreto-Ley, el que comenzará a regir a partir de su publicación en la Gaceta Oficial de la República.

DADO en el Palacio de la Revolución, en Ciudad de La Habana, a los 15 días del mes de febrero de 1982.

*Fidel Castro Ruz*

# GACETA OFICIAL
## DE LA REPUBLICA DE CUBA

EXTRAORDINARIA LA HABANA, VIERNES 1ro DE OCTUBRE DE 1982 AÑO LXXX

Imprenta: Zanja No. 352, esq. a Escobar. - Habana 2

Número 45                                                                    Página 203

## COMITES ESTATALES

---

## FINANZAS

### RESOLUCION NO. 52-82

POR CUANTO: El Decreto-Ley No. 50, de 15 de febrero de 1982, dispone en su Artículo 26, inciso a), que las empresas mixtas son sujetos del impuesto sobre utilidades, precisándose a los efectos de la determinación de la utilidad neta imponible, dietar el correspondiente Reglamento.

POR CUANTO: Las empresas mixtas, de acuerdo con lo dispuesto en el inciso b) del citado Artículo 26, son también sujetos del impuesto sobre nóminas.

POR CUANTO: El expresado Decreto-Ley No. 50 dispone en su Artículo 29 que las empresas mixtas presenten al Comité Estatal de Finanzas, en el término y las condiciones que éste establezca, los estados financieros que se les exijan, sin perjucio de las auditorías oficiales que disponga dicha Comité Estatal.

POR CUANTO: El mencionado Decreto-Ley No. 50, en su Artículo 30, establece que las partes asociadas pueden determinar libremente el sistema de contabilidad más comveniente a los fines de la asociación económica, siempre que el sistema adoptado se ajuste a los principios que universalmente se aceptan en este campo y que permita satisfacer las exigencias fiscales.

POR CUANTO: Se hace necesario dictar las disposiciones complementarias para la aplicación de los preceptos antes referidos.

POR TANTO: En uso de las facultades que me están conferidas en el inciso ñ) del Artículo 53 de la Ley 1323 de 1976,

## Resuelvo:
PRIMERO: Dictar el siguiente

## REGLAMENTO PARA LA DETERMINACION DE LAS UTILIDADES DE LAS EMPRESAS MIXTAS

ARTICULO 1.- Para la determinación de la utilidad neta, las empresas mixtas deducirán del total de los ingresos brutos obtenidos por todos los conceptos el importe de los gastos ordinarios y necesarios en que incurran o que sean realizados durante cada año natural, según lo que más adelante se regula.

## DE LOS INGRESOS

ARTICULO 2.- Se entiende por ingresos, a los efectos de la determinación de las utilidades a que se refiere el inciso a) del Artículo 26 del Decreto-Ley 50, toda percepción en dinero, en valores o en cualquier otra forma que aumente el patrimonio del contribuyente y de la que pueda disponer sin obligación de restituir su importe.

ARTICULO 3.- Se consideran ingresos, de acuerdo con lo

establecido en el artículo anterior, los realmente devengados en el período imponible, con independencia de si los mismos han sido percibidos efectivamente durante, antes o después del referido período, así como los que, no habiendo sido considerados como ingresos en períodos anteriores, por no haberse podido prever, se determinen o perciban en el período de que se trate.

Cuando se trate de ingresos correspondientes a prestaciones de cumplimiento aplazado, que abarquen más de un período imponible, se diferirá la parte del ingreso imputable a los períodos siguientes.

ARTICULO 4.- La cancelación de cualquier deuda del contribuyente por causa diferente a su pago se considera como ingreso en el período en que ocurra.

ARTICULO 5.- Las primas obtenidas en bonos, pagarés u obligaciones de cualquier naturaleza se prorratearán durante el tiempo en que estuvieren en circulación.

En caso de que dichos valores fueren cancelados, total o parcialmente, antes del vencimiento previsto, la parte de la prima que aún no hubiera sido prorrateada se considerará como ingreso del período en que se realice la cancelación.

Las primas o excesos sobre el valor nominal en la venta de acciones de la propia entidad contribuyente no se considerarán ingresos gravados por este impuesto, considerándose a todos los efectos como capital de la misma.

ARTICULO 6.- La utilidad proveniente de la venta o traspaso de propiedades, bienes y demás activos de la entidad contribuyente, así como de la revalorización de los mismos, se considerará como ingreso del período en que dichas operaciones se produzcan; salvo en el caso de las revalorizaciones que este Comité Estatal autorice deducir de los ingresos gravados.

ARTICULO 7.- El importe de las reducciones del monto de las reservas constituidas con carácter voluntario, o la liquidación de éstas, se considerarán como ingreso del año en que se efectúe dicha reducción o liquidación.

La liquidación de las reservas constituidas con carácter obligatorio también se considerarán como ingreso del año en que se efectúe dicha liquidación.

## DE LAS PARTIDAS DEDUCIBLES

ARTICULO 8.- Las partidas deducibles de los ingresos brutos obtenidos en cada período imponible deben estar anotadas en la contabilidad de la entidad contribuyente, tener el carácter de necesarias, haberse incurrido realmente en ellas y poderse probar su realización.

Se entenderá que un gasto tiene el carácter de necesario cuando sea propio de la actividad económica o negocio gravado y esté dentro de los límites normales del giro.

ARTICULO 9.- Para la determinación de las utilidades en operaciones, se deduce del importe de los ingresos brutos obtenidos en el período imponible el importe de los gastos necesarios para la obtención de dichos ingresos, determinado según los principios de contabilidad generalmente aceptados.

ARTICULO 10.- A los efectos de la determinación de sus costos, las entidades contribuyentes deberán valorizar sus inventarios al costo, utilizando cualquiera de los métodos siguientes:

a) Al precio real de compra, o al costo de la producción propia, de cada una de las partidas en existencia en la fecha de cierre;

b) al costo promedio de las compras efectuadas o de la producción propia;

c) por el método "primero en entrar, primero en salir", aplicado a las compras efectuadas o a la producción propia; y

d) por el método "ultimo en entrar, primero en salir", aplicado a las compras efectuadas o a la producción propia.

El precio de compra comprende el consignado en la factura más todos los gastos adicionales que se produzcan hasta que la mercancía esté depositada en el almacén. Tratándose de fabricación propia, el costo de producción comprenderá los gastos de las materias primas, los materiales auxiliares, la fuerza de trabajo y aquellos otros gastos que técnicamente correspondan de acuerdo con el sistema de costos empleado.

Una vez adoptado uno de los expresados métodos de valoración no se podrá cambiar el mismo sin la previa autorización de este Comité Estatal de Finanzas.

ARTICULO 11.- Las mermas en la producción y el deterioro de mercancías, envases, materias primas y materiales auxiliares son deducibles, siempre que estén dentro de los límites normales del giro o actividad correspondiente o que puedan probarse debidamente.

ARTICULO 12.- Son deducibles para la determinación de las utilidades gravadas:

a) El importe pagado por el arrendamiento de instalaciones y otros bienes.

b) Las mejoras en propiedades arrendadas o en usufructo, prorrateadas entre el número de años del contrato de arrendamiento o del derecho de usufructo, o de los años que falten por decursar de su vigencia, hasta un máximo de 5 años. Cuando se trate de activos fijos que, de acuerdo con lo establecido en el Artículo 13 de este Reglamento, tengan un término de depreciación menor que el de vigencia del contrato de arrendamiento o del derecho de usufructo, o menor de 5 años, según el caso, se aplicarán las normas de depreciación establecidas en dicho artículo.

ARTICULO 13.- Es deducible de los ingresos brutos obtenidos la depreciación de los activos fijos propios de las entidades contribuyentes, hasta los siguientes porcentajes anuales máximos sobre el valor de adquisición más los gastos en que se incurra hasta que queden totalmente instalados:

I Edificaciones y otras construcciones

a) Edificaciones:

| | |
|---|---|
| de madera solamente | 6% |
| de mampostería y otros materiales | 3% |

b) Otras construcciones:

| | |
|---|---|
| Puentes de acero, hierro u hormigón | 3% |
| Puentes de madera | 6% |
| Muelles, espigones o embarcaderos | |
| de madera | 6% |
| de estructura de hormigón reforzado o | |
| de estacas de acero | 3% |
| Diques secos y flotantes; varaderos | 6% |
| Silos y tanques | 6% |
| c) Otras no clasificadas | 3% |

II Muebles, enseres y equipos de oficina:

| | |
|---|---|
| a) Muebles y estantes | 10% |

b) Equipos de oficina:

| | |
|---|---|
| Máquinas de escribir | 15% |
| Máquinas de sumar y calcular | 15% |
| Mimeógrafos y duplicadoras | 15% |
| Adresógrafos | 15% |
| Equipos de microfilm | 15% |
| Máquinas procesadoras de datos | 25% |
| Otros equipos no clasificados | 15% |

c) Enseres:

| | |
|---|---|
| Equipos de aire acondicionado | 15% |
| Intercomunicadores | 15% |
| Otros enseres no clasificados | 10% |

III Equipos no tecnológicos:

Equipos de transporte:

| | |
|---|---|
| a) Aéreo | 25% |
| b) Marítimo | 6% |

c) Terrestre:

| | |
|---|---|
| Autos | 20% |
| Omnibus | 20% |
| Camiones | 20% |
| Camiones con equipos mezcladores | 25% |
| Rastras y cuñas | 20% |
| Motocicletas | 20% |
| Motonetas | 20% |
| Bicicletas | 20% |
| Equipos de transporte ferroviario | 6% |
| Equipos mecanizados para la construcción | 25% |
| Tractores y otros equipos agrícolas mecanizados | 25% |
| Implementos agrícolas | 15% |
| Otros no clasificados | 10% |
| IV. Maquinaria en general | 6% |

V. Animales:

| | |
|---|---|
| dedicados a la recría | 15% |
| dedicados a la producción de leche | 15% |
| dedicados a la producción de huevos | 50% |
| de trabajo | 10% |
| Otros no clasificados | 10% |

VI. Otros activos:

| | |
|---|---|
| Cercas | 10% |
| Películas y video-cassettes | 25% |
| Otros no clasificados | 5% |

ARTICULO 14.- El importe de las revalorizaciones de los activos fijos sólo es depreciable si hubiese sido oportunamente declarado como ingreso.

No se admite como gasto deducible la depreciación de terrenos, pozos, vías férreas, herramientas manuales, útiles de trabajo y libros; pero serán deducibles las minoraciones de estas partidas, con excepción de los terrenos, por razón de roturas, pérdidas físicas o deterioro.

ARTICULO 15.- Las reparaciones que realicen las entidades contribuyentes para mantener sus activos fijos en condiciones adecuadas de funcionamiento, incluidas las sustituciones de piezas o partes de dichos activos, constituyen gastos deducibles.

En el caso de sustituciones de bienes retirados, se admite como deducible la cantidad que falte por depreciar de los mismos, siempre que no se produzca su venta, caso este último en que se estará a la utilidad o pérdida producida en dicha operación.

No se incluyen en el concepto de reparación y de sustitución parcial y, por ende, son capitalizables, las reparaciones que constituyan nuevos activos o unidades adicionales a los ya existentes.

ARTICULO 16.- Son deducibles los gastos en que se incurra por el uso de patentes, diseños, procesos, fórmulas, marcas u otras formas de la propiedad industrial, así como por el uso del derecho de autor, prorrateados entre el número de años de vigencia legal, de acuerdo con el valor de costo, o con el de revalorización si ésta hubiese sido declarada como ingreso a los efectos de este impuesto. Aunque se considere, en un caso determinado, que la vida útil es inferior a la legal, no se podrá adoptar una amortización diferente a la legal, salvo autorización expresa de este Comité a solicitud de la empresa contribuyente.

ARTICULO 17.- Son deducibles los gastos de experimentación e investigación, prorrateados entre un máximo de 5 años.

ARTICULO 18.- Se considera deducible el importe de las cuentas incobrables a clientes.

ARTICULO 19.- Se consideran deducibles los importes de los gastos de viajes al extranjero realizados por los funcionarios o empleados de las entidades contribuyentes con objeto de efectuar gestiones de las mismas.

ARTICULO 20.- Se consideran deducibles los gastos de las oficinas que mantengan en el extranjero los sujetos de este impuesto, siempre que reúnan los requisitos exigidos con carácter general en este reglamento.

ARTICULO 21.- Las asignaciones que, por todos los conceptos, se fijen por las entidades contribuyentes a los miembros de sus juntas de directores o de otros grupos colegiados, o a sus socios y gerentes, tienen que reunir los siguientes requisitos, en adición a los establecidos en general por este reglamento para los demás gastos deducibles:

a) que estén acordados por los órganos competentes de la entidad, y

b) que se paguen efectivamente, o se acrediten en cuenta a los destinatarios, en el período a que se contraen.

Las gratificaciones, los gastos de representación y cualquier otra retribución por el trabajo que perciban las personas relacionadas en este artículo se computarán, a los efectos expuestos, como asignaciones a las mismas.

ARTICULO 22.- También se considera gasto deducible la amortización de los gastos de organización e instalación, prorrateados entre un máximo de 5 años.

ARTICULO 23.- Se consideran gastos deducibles los intereses sobre préstamos realizados con bancos y con instituciones oficiales, nacionales o extranjeros.

ARTICULO 24.- Se consideran deducibles los gastos de emisión y los descuentos en bonos, pagarés y obligaciones de cualquier naturaleza, prorrateados en proporción al tiempo en que estuvieren en circulación. En caso que dichos valores fueren cancelados, total o parcialmente, antes del vencimiento previsto, la parte de los descuentos y gastos que aún no haya sido amortizada, se considera como gasto del período en que se efectúe la cancelación.

ARTICULO 25.- No constituye un gasto deducible la amortización de descuentos en la venta de acciones propias de la entidad contribuyente, ni los dividendos.

Tampoco se admitirá como gasto deducible la amortización de la plusvalía o de la sobrevaloración de negocios.

ARTICULO 26.- Las pérdidas ocasionadas por cualquier clase de siniestro son deducibles en los períodos en que los mismos ocurran, después de deducidos los importes de las indemnizaciones que procedan. Si a la terminación de un período imponible no se conoce el importe exacto de las pérdidas, o el de las correspondientes indemnizaciones, se hará un estimado de los mismos, sujetos a un ajuste final en el período en que se determine su ascendencia.

ARTICULO 27.- Los gastos a que vengan obligadas legalmente las entidades contribuyentes por razón de resoluciones administrativas o judiciales correspondientes a períodos imponibles anteriores a aquél al que esté determinando la utilidad y que no hubieren sido previstos oportunamente, son deducibles de las utilidades del período siempre que reúnan los requisitos exigidos por este reglamento para ser considerados como gastos deducibles.

Igualmente, se admitirá la deducción de los gastos diferidos en períodos anteriores por corresponder a beneficios que pueden estenderse a más de un período.

ARTICULO 28.- Se consideran deducibles:

a) Los impuestos y contribuciones devengados a favor del Estado, con excepción del impuesto sobre las utilidades a que se contrae el presente reglamento;

b) el importe de las donaciones al Estado cubano.

ARTICULO 29.- De la utilidad en operaciones que resulte de la aplicación de los anteriores artículos del presente reglamento se deducirá, a los efectos del cálculo y determinación de la utilidad neta imponible, o sea, de la utilidad a la que se aplica el tipo impositivo establecido:

a) La parte de la utilidad que se reinvierta para incrementar el capital social;

b) la parte de la utilidad destinada a constitutir reservas para contingencias o con otros objetivos que hayan acordado las partes, tanto las obligatorias como las voluntarias;

c) la parte de la utilidad que se destine a los fondos de estimulación económica de los trabajadores cubanos, y

d) las pérdidas de años anteriores, prorrateadas en los 5 años inmediatamente posteriores.

ARTICULO 30.- No se admitirá como deducible partida alguna que no esté autorizada como tal por el presente reglamento, salvo aprobación expresa de este Comité Estatal de Finanzas a solicitud de parte interesada.

## DE LOS ESTADOS FINANCIEROS

ARTICULO 31.- Las empresas mixtas quedan obligadas a llevar la contabilidad de sus operaciones en idioma español y a presentar a este Comité Estatal de Finanzas:

a) Los estados financierso correspondientes a sus operaciones en cada uno de los tres primeros trimestres naturales de cada año, dentro del mes siguiente al cierre de los mismos;

b) los estados financieros correspondientes a sus operaciones de cada año natural, dentro de los dos primeros meses del año siguiente, término establecido para el pago del impuesto sobre utilidades, según el Artículo 26 del Decreto-Ley No. 50.

Los referidos estados financieros se presentarán de conformidad con los modelos que pondrá en vigor el Vicepresidente que atiende la Dirección de Ingresos de este Comité Estatal.

## DEL IMPUESTO SOBRE INGRESOS A LOS TRABAJADORES (IMPUESTOS SOBRE NOMINAS)

SEGUNDO: A los efectos del pago del impuesto sobre ingresos a los trabajadores (impuesto sobre nóminas) a que se refiere el inciso b) del Artíulo 26 del Decreto-Ley No. 50, las empresas mixtas, conjuntamente con el pago de la suma mensual, equivalente al importe total de los salarios y demás remuneraciones devengados por el personal cubano, que efectúen a la entidad cubana con la que hayan contratado la utilización de la fuerza de trabajo cubana, pagarán el equivalente del importe del impuesto antes mencionado. La entidad cubana de que se trate ingresará el equivalente del importe del impuesto al Presupuesto Central dentro de los 10 días siguientes al de su cobro.

## DEL RECARGO POR MORA

TERCERO: Las empresas mixtas que, de acuerdo con lo dispuesto en el Artículo 27 de la Ley No. 1213, de 27 de junio de 1967, incurran en mora por no satisfacer los impuestos sobre utilidades y sobre ingresos de los trabajadores (impuesto sobre nóminas) dentro de los términos establecidos para ello, deberán pagar el 10% de recargo sobre el principal adeudado, establecido por el Artículo 28 de la citada ley.

## DE LA INSCRIPCION EN EL REGISTRO DE CONTRIBUYENTES

CUARTO: Las entidades a que se refiere el apartado anterior deberán inscribirse en el Registro de Contribuyentes del Estado, que obra en el Departamento de Ingresos de la Dirección de Finanzas del Organo Municipal del Poder Popular que corresponda a su domicilio, y a tal efecto deberán presentar la solicitud de inscripción a la que acompañarán los documentos siguientes:

a) copia literal certificada de la escritura o documento de constitución de la entidad contribuyente;

b) certificación de su inscripción en el Registro de Asociaciones Económicas de la Cámara de Comercio de la República de Cuba, y

c) una certificación expedida por el Secretario de la entidad, con el visto bueno del Presidente, en la que conste los miembros que integran la junta de directores, los cargos que desempeñan y sus funciones.

A partir de su inscripción en el Registro de Contribuyentes, las entidades en cuestión deberán hacer constar el número de inscripción que les haya correspondido en dicho Registro en toda clase de escrito o documento que deban presentar en cualquier entidad estatal cubana.

QUINTO: Publíquese en la Gaceta Oficial de la República para general conocimiento y archívese el original en la Dirección de Asesoría Jurídica de este Comité.

DADA en la Ciudad de La Habana, a los 15 días del mes de septiembre de 1982.

**Francisco García Valls**
*Ministro-Presidente*
*Comité Estatal de Finanzas*

---

## RESOLUCION NO. 53-82

POR CUANTO: El Decreto-Ley No. 50, de 15 de febrero de 1982, dispone en su Artículo 22 que las empresas mixtas contituyan, con cargo a sus utilidades, una reserva para cubrir las contingencias que pudieran producirse en sus operaciones, dentro de los límites y con arreglo a las regulaciones que establezca este Comité; y en su Artículo 26, inciso a), autoriza a dichas empresas a constituir otras reservas con los objetivos que acuerden las partes.

POR CUANTO: Se hace necesario establecer las normas para la formación, utilización y liquidación de las expresadas reservas.

POR TANTO: En uso de las facultades que me están conferidas en el inciso ñ) del Artículo 53 de la Ley 1323 de 1976,

### R e s u e l v o:

PRIMERO: Las empresas mixtas constituirán, con carácter obligatorio, una reserva para contingencias que se formará con un 5% de las utilidades anuales obtenidas en operaciones, hasta alcanzar una cantidad igual al 15% del capital social pagado cuando se trate de una empresa dedicada a la producción de bienes, o al 20% del capital social pagado cuando se trate de una empresa dedicada a la prestación de servicios.

SEGUNDO: La reserva para contingencias sólo podrá ser utilizada para cubrir pérdidas u otras contingencias, y el monto utilizado se deberá restituir mediante la aplicación del 10% a las utilidades que se obtengan en operaciones.

TERCERO: Sin perjuicio de la reserva para contingencias, referida en los apartados anteriores, las empresas mixtas podrán constituir otras reservas con carácter voluntario, hasta el limite y con los objetivos que acuerde la empresa en cuestión.

CUARTO: Al disolverse la empresa mixta, las reservas constituidas, después de deducido el pago del correspondiente impuesto sobre utilidades, serán distribuidas entre las partes en la misma forma que la empresa tenga establecida para la distribución de las utilidades.

QUINTO: Publíquese en la Gaceta Ofical de la República para general conocimiento y archívese el original en la Dirección de Asesoría Jurídica de este Comité.

Dada en la Ciudad de La Habana, a los 15 días del mes de septiembre de 1982.

*Francisco García Valls*
*Ministro-Presidente*
*Comité Estatal de Finanzas*

---

## RESOLUCION No. 54-82

POR CUANTO: El Decreto-Ley No. 50, de 15 de febrero de 1982, establece en su Artículo 18 que las empresas mixtas arrendatarias o usufructuarias de instalaciones industriales, turísticas o de cualquier tipo, aseguran dichas instalaciones a favor del arrendador cubano o del que hace el aporte.

POR CUANTO: La Ley No. 1323, de 30 de noviembre de 1976, establece en su Artículo 60, inciso e), como una de las atribuciones y funciones principales de este Comité, la de dirigir la actividad del seguro estatal.

POR TANTO: En uso de las facultades que me están conferidas en el inciso ñ) del Artículo 53 de la referida Ley 1323,

### R e s u e l v o:

PRIMERO: Disponer que las instalaciones industriales, turísticas o de cualquier tipo que sean dadas en arrendamiento o en usufructo por empresas y otras organizaciones nacionales a empresas mixtas, sean aseguradas por estas últimas, a favor de las primeras, contra los siguientes riesgos o contingencias:

a) Incendio y/o rayo;

b) huracán, ciclón, tornado y manga de viento,

c) desbordamiento del mar o inundación, cualquiera que sea la causa que lo origine, y

d) en las zonas sísmicas, contra terremoto e incendio como consecuencia de terremoto.

SEGUNDO: Publíquese en la Gaceta Oficial de la República para general conocimiento y archívese el original en la Dirección de Asesoría Jurídica de este Comité.

Dada en la Ciudad de La Habana, a los 15 días del mes de septiembre de 1982.

*Francisco García Valls*
*Ministro-Presidente*
*Comité Estatal de Finanzas*

---

## PRECIOS
## RESOLUCION NO. M - 24/82

POR CUANTO: El Decreto-Ley No. 50, de 15 de febrero de 1982, define en su Artículo 32 las operaciones respecto a las cuales las empresas estatales cubanas tendrán el derecho de primera opción sobre la base de que ofrezcan a las empresas mixtas, o a las partes de las demás formas de asociación económica en los casos procedentes, precios y demás condiciones competitivas a escala internacional.

POR CUANTO: El propio Decreto-Ley, en su Artículo 34, inciso b), establece que las empresas estatales cubanas garantizarán a las empresas mixtas, y a las partes de las demás formas de asociación económica en los casos procedentes, mediante contrato, la prestación de los servicios no obtenibles por vía de comercio exterior.

POR CUANTO: La Ley No. 1323, de 30 de noviembre de 1976, dispone en su Artículo 62 inciso b), que correponde al Comité Estatal de Precios establecer las normas y metodologías que regulen la formación, fijación, modificación, publicación y control de los precios y tarifas.

POR TANTO: En uso de las facultades que me están conferidas en el inciso ñ) del Artículo 53 de la referida Ley 1323,

### Resuelvo:

PRIMERO: Las empresas estatales cubanas no estarán sujetas a lo establecido en materia de precios por este Comité Estatal cuando contraten con empresas mixtas o con las partes de otras formas de asociación económica:

a) el suministro al por mayor de combustible, materias primas, materailes, productos intermedios, herramientas, equipos, piezas de repuesto, accesorios y bienes de consumo:

b) la compra de la producción terminada o del servicio que preste la asociación económica;

c) el transporte de carga internacional;

d) el seguro de bienes e instalaciones.

SEGUNDO: Las empresas estatales cubanas que contraten con empresas mixtas o con las partes de otras formas de asociación económica el suministro de energía eléctrica, gas doméstico y agua; el servicio de teléfonos y teletipos locales e internacionales; el transporte nacional y los demás servicios relacionados en el anexo de esta resolución, aplicarán las tarifas oficiales que en cada caso se mencionan en dicho anexo, las cuales estarán vigentes a estos fines hasta el 31 de diciembre de 1983.

Cuando se trate de la prestación de servicios no repetitivos no contemplados en las Listas Oficiales de Precios, las empresas estatales se atendrán, para la formación del precio, a lo establecido en la Instrucción Metodológica No. 141 de este Comité Estatal.

TERCERO: Se derogan cuantas disposiciones de igual o inferior rango se opongan al cumplimiento de lo que por la presente se dispone, la que comenzará a regir a partir de la fecha de su publicación.

CUARTO: Notifíquese a los organismos de la Administración Central del Estado, así como a cuantas demás personas naturales o jurídicas proceda. Archívese el original en la Asesoría Jurídica de este Comité y publíquese en la Gaceta Oficial de la República para general conocimiento.

DADA en la Ciudad de La Habana, a los 15 días del mes de septiembre de 1982.

**Antonio Rodríguez Maurell**
*Ministro-Presidente*
*Comité Estatal de Precios*

## TARIFAS DE SERVICIOS
## APLICABLES A LAS ASOCIACIONES ECONOMICAS
### —Vigentes hasta el 31 de diciembre, 1983 —

| | No. de la lista oficial de precios (LOP) | Establecida mediante resolución | Fecha de la resolución | Vigente a partir de |
|---|---|---|---|---|
| Energía eléctrica | 01.01.00.01 | PR-248-80 | 2 mayo 80 | 1 enero 81 |
| Adición | 01.01.00.01 | AP-623-31 | 17 Nov.81 | 17 Nov. 81 |
| Gas licuado (doméstico) | 01.02.02.02 | PP-171-79 | 24 Jul. 79 | 1 enero 81 |
| Abasto de agua | 01.21.05.01 | PR-860-80 | 25 Dic. 80 | 1 enero 81 |
| Teléfono | 06.00.00.01 | PR-860-80 | 25 Dic. 80 | 1 enero 81 |
| Adición | 06.00.00.01 | P -348-81 | 10 abril 81 | 10 abril 81 |
| Télex internacional | 06.00.00.01 | PR-860-80 | 25 Dic. 80 | 1 enero 81 |
| Adición | 06.00.00.01 | PR-783-80 | 2 Dic. 80 | 1 enero 81 |
| Adición | 06.00.00.01 | P-98-81 | 10 Feb. 81 | 10 Feb. 81 |
| Telégrafo | 06.00.00.02 | PR-860-80 | 25 Dic. 80 | 1 enero 81 |
| Transporte terrestre de carga general | 05.00.00.01 | PR-860-80 | 25 Dic. 80 | 1 enero 81 |
| Modificación | 05.00.00.01 | PR-925-80 | 31 Dic. 80 | 1 enero 81 |
| Rectificación | 05.00.00.01 | P-52-81 | 30 enero 81 | 30 enero 81 |
| Alquiler de equipos portacontenedores | 05.00.00.01 | PR-782-80 | 2 Dic. 80 | 1 enero 81 |
| Transporte ferroviario | 05.01.00.01 | PR-860-80 | 25 Dic. 80 | 1 enero 81 |
| Modificación | 05.00.00.01 | PR-925-80 | 31 Dic. 80 | 1 enero 81 |
| Rectificación | 05.01.00.01 | P-53-81 | 30 enero 81 | 30 enero 81 |
| Transporte por camiones | 05.02.03.01 | PR-860-80 | 25 Dic. 80 | 1 enero 81 |
| Rectificación | 05.02.03.01 | P-54-81 | 30 enero 81 | 30 enero 81 |
| Recogida de basura | 05.02.03.01 | AP-200-81 | 15 Jul 81 | 15 Jul. 81 |
| Carga a granel en camión de volteo (tarifa coordinada) | 05.00.00.04 | PR-860-80 | 25 Dic. 80 | 1 enero 81 |
| Adición | 05.00.00.04 | P-114-81 | 16 Feb. 81 | 16 Feb. 81 |
| Carga a granel en camión devolteo (transporte específico) | 05.02.03.06 | P-115-81 | 16 Feb. 81 | 16 Feb. 81 |
| Transporte de cabotaje marítimo y fluvial | 05.04.02.01 | PR-860-80 | 25 Dic. 80 | 1 enero 81 |
| Servicios conexos del transporate marítimo | 05.04.03.01 | PR-860-80 | 25 Dic. 80 | 1 enero 81 |
| Actividades de carga y descarga | 05.06.01.01 | PR-860-80 | 25 Dic. 80 | 1 enero 81 |
| Actividad de expedición | 05.06.02.01 | PR-860-80 | 25 Dic. 80 | 1 enero 81 |

## TRABAJO Y SEGURIDAD SOCIAL
## RESOLUCION No. 1647

POR CUANTO: El Decreto-Ley No. 50, de 15 de febreo de 1982, establece en sus artículos 36 al 42 el régimen laboral que debe regir las relaciones entre los trabajadores cubanos que presten servicios en una empresa mixta, ésta y la entidad cubana empleadora.

POR CUANTO: Resulta conveniente precisar algunos aspectos relacionados con los derechos y obligaciones que nacen para la entidad cubana que facilitará la fuerza de trabajo a la empresa mixta y para ésta en relación con dichos trabajadores y con la entidad empleadora.

POR CUANTO: La Ley No. 1323, de 30 de noviembre de 1976, establece en su Artículo 63 que el Comité Estatal de Trabajo y Seguridad Social es el organismo encargado de dirigir y controlar la aplicación de la política del Estado y del Gobierno en materia laboral.

POR TANTO: En uso de las facultades que me están conferidas en el inciso ñ) del Artículo 53 de la referida Ley 1323,

### R e s u e l v o:

PRIMERO: La entidad cubana empleadora y la empresa mixta pactarán en el contrato que suscriban - o las partes en el covenio de asociación, si la entidad cubana empleadora fuese parte de la empresa mixta - el número de trabajadores de todas la categorías ocupacionales que la primera facilitará a la segunda, especificando cuántas plazas van a ser cubiertas de cada ocupación o cargo, el carácter permanente o eventual de las mismas y la oportunidad en que esa fuerza de trabajo seá suministrada.

SEGUNDO: El personal que suministrará la entidad cubana empleadora para cubrir las plazas a que se refiere el apartado primero deberá ser aprobado por la empresa mixta.

Si se tratase de centros de trabajo existentes antes de la constitución de la empresa mixta, la selección del personal deberá respetar los derechos escalafonarios anteriormente vigentes en dicho centro, según lo dispuesto por la Resolución No. 70, de 30 de noviembre de 1977, de este Comité Estatal.

TERCERO: Los trabajadores cubanos que laboren en la empresa mixta acatarán la disciplina y la organización que rijan en la misma. A esos efectos, la entidad cubana empleadora, de acuerdo con la empresa mixta, establecerá las normas disciplinarias pertinentes y las pondrá en conocimiento de los trabajadores que presten servicio en dicha empresa.

CUARTO: Cuando la empresa mixta no pueda mantener en su plantilla a uno o varios trabajadores suministrados por la entidad cubana empleadora, ya sea porque no reúnan los requisitos del cargo u ocupación que desempeñen, carezcan de idoneidad para el mismo, violen la disciplina laboral, o bien porque se trate de amortización de plazas o de una interrupción laboral de más de 30 días, o porque exista cualquiera otra causa que justifique tal decisión, comunicará este particular a la entidad cubana, la que asumirá en lo adelante la responsabilidad que correponda sobre tales trabajadores, a los cuales aplicará la legislación vigente para cada una de las diferentes situaciones planteadas.

En el caso de las interrupciones de hasta 30 días, la empresa mixta no devolverá el trabajador a la entidad cubana empleadora, y se abonará al interrupto, a cuenta de la empresa mixta, la garantía salarial que corresponda, en los términos y condiciones establecidos en la legislación vigente.

Cuando se trate de la amortización de plazas o de una interrupción laboral de más de 30 días, la declaración de disponibles o de interruptos, según el caso, se hará respetando los derechos escalafonarios vigentes en el centro de trabajo en cuestión.

QUINTO: Cuando la empresa mixta comunique la devolución de un trabajador por alguna de las causas a que se refiere el apartado anterior, o si es el trabajador el que da por cancelada la relación laboral, la entidad cubana empleadora viene obligada a sustituir al referido trabajador, salvo que se trate de la amortización de plazas o de una interrupción laboral.

SEXTO: Sobre la base de las tarifas y demás regulaciones del Sistema Salarial oficialmente establecido en el país, la empresa cubana empleadora y la empresa mixta acordarán en el contrato que suscriban - o, en su caso, las partes en el convenio de asociación - las formas y sístemas de pago específicos, así como el procedimiento de confección de nóminas, que se aplicarán en la empresa en cuestión.

La entidad cubana empleadora, de acuerdo con la empresa mixta, establecerá el reglamento de primas aplicabale a los trabajadores que laboren en dicha empresa, en el marco de lo dispuesto en el

Reglamento General de primas dictado mediante el Decreto No. 50 del Comité Ejecutivo del Consejo de Ministros, de 19 de octubre de 1979.

Conforme a lo establecido en el Artículo 41 del Decreto-Ley No. 50, los salarios del personal dirigente cubano son convenidos por las partes de la asociación económica en correspondencia con el salario asignado al personal dirigente extranjero.

SEPTIMO: El personal cubano que labore en la empresa mixta disfrutará de las vacaciones anuales pagadas que le concede la legislación vigente.

El momento de disfrute de dichas vacaciones será determinado por la empresa mixta en el marco de lo establecido en el Decreto No. 81 del Comité Ejecutivo del Consejo de Ministros, de 10 de marzo de 1981.

OCTAVO: La empresa mixta reembolsará a la entidad cubana empleadora, dentro de los tres días hábiles siguientes a cada período de pago de nómina, el importe de todas las remuneraciones que haya devengado el personal cubano en dicho período, ya sea trabajando o disfrutando de las vacaciones anuales pagadas.

NOVENO: El personal cubano que labora en la empresa mixta disfrutará igualmente de los beneficios de la Seguridad Social que le concede la legislación vigente.

El pago del impuesto sobre nóminas a que viene obligada la empresa mixta según lo dispuesto en el inciso b) del Artículo 26 del Decreto-Ley No. 50 cubre todas las obligaciones económicas de dicha empresa por este concepto, las cuales no tienen que ser reflejadas en el contrato ni, en su caso, en el convenio de asociación.

DECIMO: La entidad cubana empleadora y la empresa mixta también reflejarán en el contrato - o, en su caso, las partes en el covenio de asociación, - la cuantía de los aportes anuales que hará esta última al fondo de estimulación económica a los trabajadores cubanos a que se refiere el Artículo 42 del Decreto-Ley No. 50, según lo que a ese respecto haya determinado la Comisión mencionada en el Artículo 1 del propio Decreto-Ley No. 50.

Los aportes correspondientes a un año dado serán transferidos por la empresa mixta a la entidad cubana empleadora dentero de los tres primeros meses del siguiente año, y la entidad cubana hará la distribución entre los trabajadores dentro de los tres días hábiles siguientes.

UNDECIMO: La empresa mixta está obligada a ofrecer condiciones de trabajo seguras e higiénicas a los trabajadores que laboren en la misma, de conformidad con lo establecido en la legislación vigente sobre la materia y asumiendo los gastos en que deba incurrir por este concepto.

DUODECIMO: Las reclamaciones que puedan presentar los trabajadores que laboren en la empresa mixta en relación con sus derechos laborales se ventilarán con la entidad cubana empleadora de conformidad con lo establecido en la legislación vigente para el resto de los trabajadores del país.

DECIMOTERCERO: Los contratos de trabajo individuales que suscribirá la entidad cubana empleadora con los trabajadores cubanos no dirigentes que laboren en la empresa mixta deberán amparar todos los deberes y derechos a que se refieren los apartados precedentes de esta resolución.

DECIMOCUARTO: La entidad cubana empleadora, o la empresa mixta, según el caso, podrán ser objeto de inspección en materia laboral y de protección e higiene del trabajo con arreglo a lo establecido en la legislación vigente en cuanto a la Inspección Nacional del Trabajo.

DECIMOQUINTO: En las zonas de alta significación para el turismo internacional que autoriza la Ley No. 33 de 10 de enero de 1981 se establecerá el régimen laboral especial que en cada caso se determine por este organismo en coordinación con el Instituto Nacional de Turismo y la Central de Trabajadores de Cuba, para lo cual se tomarán en consideración los factores geográficos, sociales y económicos de cada zona.

DECIMOSEXTO: Publíquese en la Gaceta Oficial de la República para general conocimiento.

DADA en la Ciudad de La Habana, a los 15 días del mes de septiembre de 1982.

*Joaquín Benavides Rodríguez*
*Ministro-Presidente*
*Comité Estatal de Trabajo y*
*Seguridad Social*

## BANCO NACIONAL DE CUBA
### RESOLUCIÓN NO. 659

POR CUANTO: El Decreto-Ley No. 50, de 15 de febreo de 1982, establece en su Artículo 44 que los trabajadores extranjeros de las empresas mixtas y demás formas de asociación económica puedan remesar al exterior el por cineto de sus salarios en divísas convertibles que determine el Banco Nacional de Cuba.

POR CUANTO: El artículo 33 de la Ley No. 1323 de 30 de noviembre de 1976, Ley de Organización de la Administración Central de Estado, dispone que los Jefes de Organismos de la Administración Central del Estado son sustituidos temporalmente, cuando fuese necesario, por los Vicepresidentes Primero o Viceministros Primero.

POR CUANTO: Por acuerdo del 23 de enero de 1978 del Consejo de Estado, se designó al que resuelve, Vicepresidente Primero del Banco Nacional de Cuba.

POR TANTO: En uso de las facultades que me están confereidas en el inciso ñ) del Artículo 53 de la Ley número 1323, de 30 de noviembre de 1976,

### R e s u e l v o:

PRIMERO: El personal extranjero que preste servicios en una empresa mixta o a alguna de las partes de otra forma de asociación económica podrá, a su conveniencia, remesar al exterior hasta el 66% de los haberes que perciba de su empleador.

SEGUNDO: Se consideran parte de dichos haberes el sueldo y las demás remuneraciones que por cualquier concepto perciba el personal extranjero por el desempeño de su trabajo en la empresa mixta o para alguna de las partes de otra forma de asociación económica.

TERCERO: Esos haberes serán depositados por el empleador en cuenta corriente abierta a nombre del trabajador extranjero de que se trate en el Banco Nacional de Cuba o en otro banco del sistema.

CUARTO: Para hacer sus remesas al exterior, el trabajador extranjero girará contra su cuenta corriente mediante solicitud que presentará en los modelos oficiales del Banco.

QUINTO: El trabajador extranjero podrá transferir a cuenta de ahorro, o a depósito a plazo fijo, el por ciento remesable de sus haberes. Los fondos de esa cuenta o depósito, incluídos los intereses que devenguen, estarán a la libre disposición del depositante conforme a las regulaciones que norman dichas cuentas y depósitos.

COMUNIQUESE: A los Vicepresidentes del Banco Nacional de Cuba y a los organismos de la Administración Central del Estado, y archívese el original en Secretaría.

PUBLIQUESE en la Gaceta Oficial de la República de Cuba para general conocimiento.

DADA en la Ciudad de La Habana, a los 15 días del mes de septiembre de 1982.

**Osvaldo Fuentes Torres**
*Presidente p.s.l.*

---

## RESOLUCION No. 660

POR CUANTO: El Decreto-Ley No. 50, de 15 de febrero de 1982, establece en su Artículo 21 que las empresas mixtas o las partes de otras formas de asociación económica pueden concertar préstamos en moneda extranjera, con un banco del sistema bancario nacional, o con bancos en el exterior, con arreglo a las regulaciones del Banco Nacional de Cuba sobre esta materia.

POR CUANTO: El Banco Nacional de Cuba está en disposición de colaborar con las empresas mixtas y las partes de otras formas de asociación económica que se establezcan en el país con los fines de promover y expandir las exportaciones y el turismo extranjero.

POR CUANTO: El Artículo 33 de la Ley No. 1323 de 30 de noviembre de 1976, Ley de Organización de la Administración Central del Estado, dispone que los Jefes de Organismos de la Administración Central del Estado son sustituidos temporalmelnte, cuando fuese necesario, por los Vicepresidentes Primero o Viceministros Primeros.

POR CUANTO: Por acuerdo del 23 de enero de 1978 del Consejo de Estado, se designó al que resuelve, Vicepresidente Primero del Banco Nacional de Cuba.

POR TANTO: En uso de las facultades que me están confereidas en el inciso ñ) del Artículo 53 de la Ley número 1323, de 30 de noviembre de 1976,

**R e s u e l v o:**

PRIMERO: Las empresas mixtas y las partes de otras formas de asociación económica podrán procurar financiamiento de instituciones de crédito en el exterior con el propósito de asegurar el buen desenvolvimiento de sus actividades. El Banco Nacional de Cuba, u otro banco del sistema, podrán considerar la posibilidad de brindar su respaldo en forma de garantía, o cualquier otra, para facilitar la obtención de esos créditos.

SEGUNDO: El Banco Nacional de Cuba u otro banco del sistema, asimismo, podrá brindar a las empresas mixtas y a las partes de otras formas de asociación económica facilidades crediticias para cubrir sus necesidades financieras en especial cuando se trate de complementar los recursos captados por estas últimas en el mercado internacional.

TERCERO: Los préstamos otorgados por el Banco Nacional de Cuba u otro banco del sistema serán, como norma general, por períodos hasta de un año, pero en casos especiales se considerarán solicitudes de crédito por períodos mayores. En los casos de préstamos para inversiones se considerarán períodos mayores, de acuerdo a la práctica internacional y a los méritos del proyecto de que se trate.

CUARTO: Al otorgar créditos, el Banco Nacional de Cuba u otro banco del sistema valorarán en todos los casos, que exista una adecuada correspondencia entre los recursos propios de la empresa mixta o las partes de otras formas de asociación económica y la cuantía de los préstamos bancarios requeridos.

QUINTO: Las empresas mixtas y las partes de otras formas de asociación económica asegurarán con la Empresa de Seguros Internacionales de Cuba (ESICUBA) los inventarios de materias primas, productos en proceso o terminados y otros bienes que garanticen los préstamos concedidos por el Banco Nacional de Cuba u otro banco del sistema. Los riesgos a cubrir por el seguro serán acordados casuísticamente. Se designará como beneficiario del seguro al propio beneficiario del crédito o al banco, o a ambos, según el caso.

SEXTO: El interés que fija el Banco Nacional de Cuba u otro banco del sistema se basa en las tasas internacionales para la moneda y el término de que se trate. No obstante, en determinado caso se podrá estudiar la concesión de tasas preferenciales con arreglo a la práctica vigente en los países que concurren al mercado internacional para el tipo de operación de que se trate.

SEPTIMO: El beneficiario del crédito deberá suministrar al Banco Nacional de Cuba u otro banco del sistema, mientras se mantengan vigentes las facilidades otorgadas, toda aquella información relacionada con la actividad de la asociación económica que requiera el banco para evaluar la situación financiera de esta última.

OCTAVO: El Banco Nacional de Cuba, u otro banco del sistema, pondrá a disposición de las empresas mixtas y de las partes de otras formas de asociación económica todos los servicios bancarios que habitualmente presta, tanto en el orden doméstico como en el internacional, y en este último, fundamentalmente, en lo referente a la emisión de giros y órdenes de pago, aperturas de cartas de crédito, tramitación de cobranzas documentarias, operaciones de compra y venta de monedas, coberturas para operaciones de futuro, servicios de información que se requieran y cualquier otra operación que habitualmente efectúa la banca internacional.

NOVENO: El Banco Nacional de Cuba u otro banco del sistema podrá conceder líneas de crédito a las empresas mixtas o las partes de otras formas de asociación económica para la realización de sus ventas al exterior.

DECIMO: Ni el Banco Nacional de Cuba ni otro banco del sistema concederá préstamos a la parte extranjera para su aportación al capital social de la empresa mixta o a otra forma de asociación económica.

DECIMOPRIMERO: Ni el Banco Nacional de Cuba ni otro banco del sistema otorgará préstamos en dólares estadounidenses, ni autorizará la obtención de préstamos en el exterior en esta moneda, mientras se mantengan vigentes las actuales regulaciones del Departamento del Tesoro de los Estados Unidos de América respecto a Cuba.

DECIMOSEGUNDO: No se aplicarán a las empresas mixtas, ni a las partes de otras formas de asociación económica, las normas de crédito vigentes para las empresas estatales del comercio exterior.

COMUNIQUESE: A los Vicepresidentes del Banco Nacional de Cuba, a los organismos de la Administración Central del Estado y archívese el original en Secretaría.

PUBLIQUESE en la Gaceta Oficial de la República de Cuba para su conocimiento general.

DADA en la Ciudad de La Habanas, a los 15 días del mes de septiembre de 1982.

*Osvaldo Fuentes Torres*
*President p.s.l.*

## DIRECCION GENERAL DE ADUANAS
### RESOLUCION No. 1-82

POR CUANTO: El Decreto-Ley No. 50 de 15 de febrero de 1982, establece en su Artículo 31 que las empresas mixtas, y las partes de las demás formas de asociación económica, tienen derecho a exportar su producción directamente, y a importar, también directamente, lo necesario para sus fines.

POR CUANTO: Se hace necesario establecer las regulaciones aduaneras aplicables a esas operaciones.

POR TANTO: En uso de las facultades que me están conferidas,

### R e s u e l v o:

Dictar el siguiente

### PROCEDIMIENTO PARA EL DESPACHO ADUANERO DE LAS EXPORTACIONES E IMPORTACIONES DE LAS EMPRESAS MIXTAS O DE LAS PARTES DE LAS DEMAS FORMAS DE ASOCIACION ECONOMICA

### CAPITULO I
### DE LAS EXPORTACIONES

ARTICULO 1.- Para efectuar una exportación de carácter comercial, la empresa mixta o una de las partes de otra forma de asociación económica regida por el Decreto-Ley 50 (en lo adelante "el exportador") presentará a la aduana del puerto o aeropuerto por donde vaya a llevarse a cabo dicha exportación los siguientes documentos, sin omisiones ni tachaduras:

a) La hoja de declaración de exportación, en original y cuatro copias;

b) una copia de la factura comercial, y

c) una copia de la lista de empaque, en su caso.

ARTICULO 2.- Cuando se trate de exportaciones sin carácter comercial, el exportador deberá presentar en el Departamento de Despacho Mercantil de la Oficina Central de la Dirección General de Aduanas lo siguientes documentos, sin omisiones ni tachaduras:

a) Una carta-solicitud de envío de las mercancías, en original y copia, conteniendo los siguientes datos:

- aduana del puerto o aeropuerto por donde se pretende realizar la exportación;

- tipo de producto;

- cantidad y peso de los bultos;

- carácter de la exportación (donación, muestra, obsequio y otro).

b) el permiso de exportación sin carácter comercial, en original y 4 copias.

ARTICULO 3.- Además de lo expresado en los artículos 1 ó 2, según el caso, el exportadr deberá:

a) Marcar correctamente los bultos que van a ser exportados;

b) cumplir las normas vigentes en materia sanitaria y veterinaria, así como las relativas a cargas inflamables, peligrosas o de fácil descomposición.

## CAPITULO II
## DE LAS IMPORTACIONES

ARTICULO 4.- Para efectuar una importación con carácter comercial, la empresa mixta o una de las partes de otra forma de asociación económica (en lo adelante "el importador") presentará a la aduana del puerto o aeropuerto por donde vaya a llevarse a cabo dicha importación los siguientes documentos, sin omisiones ni tachaduras:

a) La hoja de declaración de entrada de mercancías (aforo y liquidación) en original y 3 copias;

b) el conocimiento de embarque o la guía aérea original, según el caso;

c) la factura comercial original;

d) la lista de empaque original, en su caso.

ARTICULO 5.- Cuando se trate de importaciones sin carácter comercial, el importador deberá presentar en el Departamento de Despacho Mercantil de la Oficina Central de la Dirección General de Aduanas los siguientes documentos, sin omisiones ni tachaduras:

a) Una carta-solicitud de extracción de los artículos en original y copia, conteniendo los siguientes datos;

- aduana del puerto o aeropuerto donde se encuentra el

embarque;

- nombre del barco, en su caso;
- número del conocimiento de embarque o de la guía aérea, según el caso;
- tipo de producto;
- cantidad y peso de los bultos;
- carácter de la importación (donación, muestra, obsequio u otro);

b) el conocimiento de embarque o la guía aérea original, según el caso;

c) la factura comercial original;

d) la lista de empaque original, en su caso.

ARTICULO 6.- Además de lo expresado en los artículos 4 ó 5, según el caso, el importador deberá:

a) Llevar a cabo las rectificaciones pertinentes cuando los datos reflejados en los documentos a presentar no coincidan entre sí o no estén en correspondencia con el manifiesto de carga;

b) cumplir las normas vigentes en materia sanitaria y veterinaria, así como las relativas a cargas inflamables, peligrosas o de fácil descomposición;

c) liquidar los derechos arancelarios correspondientes, de acuerdo con lo establecido en el Decreto No. 227 de 23 de enero de 1958 o en las demás disposiciones legales vigentes sobre la materia; o presentar el documento acreditativo de la exención concedida por el Comité Estatal de Finanzas; o ambas cosas, si se tratase de una exención parcial;

d) extraer del recinto aduanal la mercancía importada, en los siguientes plazos:

- las cargas inflamables, peligrosas o de fácil descomposición, dentro de las 24 horas posteriores a su descarga;

- otras cargas, dentro de los 10 días hábiles siguientes a la determinación de la tarja y clasificación.

ARTICULO 7.- De acuerdo con lo establecido en las Disposiciones Generales del Arancel de Aduanas vigentes, está prohibida la importación de los productos relacionados en el anexo de esta Resolución, el cual es parte integrante de la misma.

## DISPOSICIONES ESPECIALES

PRIMERA: El despacho de las importaciones por vía postal; el de las importaciones que se hagan con carácter temporal para ser posteriormente reexportadas, así como el de los equipos que se exporten temporalmente para ser reparados en el extranjero y posteriormente reimportados, se efectúa según lo establecido en la Ley No. 1092 de 5 de febrero de 1963, de Procedimiento Aduanal, y en su Reglamento, el Decreto Presidencial número 3278, de igual fecha.

SEGUNDA: Las importaciones sin carácter comercial que haga el personal extranjero de las empresas mixtas se ajustarán a lo establecido en el Decreto-Ley No. 22, de 16 de abril de 1979 y, en el caso específico de los vehículos automotores, con arreglo a lo dispuesto en el Decreto No. 40 del Comité Ejecutivo del Consejo de Ministros, de 22 de febrero de 1979, para los técnicos extranjeros que se encuentren en Cuba en virtud de convenios o contratos de asistencia técnica.

Se derogan cuantas disposiciones administrativas se opongan a lo dispuesto en la presente Resolución, que comenzará a regir en fecha de su publicación en la Gaceta Oficial de la República.

DADA en la Ciudad de La Habana, a los 15 días del mes de septiembre de 1982.

*Oscar Carreño Gómez*
*Director General de Aduanas*

### ANEXO

_   Armas de fuego y armas blancas de cualquier tipo.

_   La dinamita, polvora y explosivos en general.

_   Los productos famacéuticos y medicinales de composición o fórmulas no registradas en la Inspección General de Farmacia.

_   Las drogas heroicas, los estupefacientes, anestésicos y extractos de alcaloides, salvo cuando sean importados por laboratorios legalmente establecidos en el territorio nacional, conforme a las disposiciones especiales de la materia.

_   Los productos alimenticios, o los destinados a la preservación de alimentos, que a juicio del Ministerio de Salud Pública no se ajusten a las disposiciones vigentes sobre la pureza de los alimentos.

_ Animales, plantas, semillas, productos vegetales y tierras, declarados dañinos, así como aquellos que pudieran ser portadores o contener gérmenes o parásitos perjudiciales.

_ El heno o cualquier otro producto sobrante de los buques que conduzcan ganado.

_ El vino artificial que no sea producto medicinal, y los vinos adulterados en cualquier forma.

_ Los perros de todas clases, no inmunizados contra la rabia o hidrofobia.

_ Los libros, pinturas, grabados, publicacciones, figuras y otros objetos obscenos y ofensivos a la moral; billetes de lotería y papeletas, talonarios, tarjetas o impresos de rifas extranjeras; y anuncios imitando monedas, billetes de banco, sellos de correos y otros valores oficiales.

_ Cualquier clase de artículo cuya importación esté prohibida por acuerdos internacioneles de los que Cuba sea parte.

## CAMARA DE COMERCIO DE CUBA

### RESOLUCION No. 6-82

POR CUANTO: El Decreto-Ley No. 50, de 15 de febrero de 1982, establece en su Artículo 10 que las empresas mixtas adquieren personalidad jurídica, y que los contratos de asociación que instrumentan otras formas de asociación económica entran en vigor cuando son inscriptos en el registro que sobre tales actividades organiza y regula la Cámara de Comercio de la República de Cuba.

POR CUANTO: Resulta necesario crear y regular el funcionamiento de este registro.

POR TANTO: En uso de las facultades que me están conferidas,

**R e s u e l v o:**

Dictar el siguiente

## REGLAMENTO DEL REGISTRO DE ASOCIACIONES ECONOMICAS

ARTICULO 1.- Se crea en la Cámara de Comercio de la República de Cuba el Registro de Asociaciones Económicas, denominado en lo adelante "el Registro".

ARTICULO 2.- El Registro contará con un Registrador y un Registrador Suplente, designados por el que resuelve.

ARTICULO 3.- Las oficinas del Registro estarán abiertas al público todos los días hábiles, en el horario que fijará el Registrador, el que lo publicará por medio de anuncio en las propias oficinas.

ARTICULO 4.- De acuerdo con lo dispuesto en el Artículo 10 del Decreto-Ley No. 50, la inscripción en el Registro es obligatoria para las empresas mixtas y formas restantes de asociación económica que se constituyan al amparo de lo dispuesto en el referido Decreto-Ley.

ARTICULO 5.- En el Registro se llevará un sello con el emblema de la Cámara de Comercio de la República de Cuba en el centro y con la siguiente inscripción "REGISTRO DE ASOCIACIONES ECONOMICAS".

El sello será fijado en todo documento que haya surtido efecto en el Registro, así como en los documentos que procedan del propio Registro.

ARTICULO 6.- En el Registro se llevarán los siguientes libros:

a) El libro diario de presentación de documentos;

b) el libro de empresas mixtas;

c) el libro de otras formas de asociaciones económicas;

d) todos aquellos otros que dispusiera el Registrador.

ARTICULO 7.- Los libros que se llevarán en el Registro de acuerdo con lo establecido en el artículo precedente deberán ser habilitados debidamente, en su primera página, por el Registrado.

ARTICULO 8.- Se considerará que forman parte del Registro todos los documentos que aparezcan archivados en el expediente o legajo que mande a formar el Registrador para cada empresa mixta o contrato de asociación que se inscriba.

ARTICULO 9.- A los efectos de las inscripciones en el Registro, se entiende por título el documento auténtico con las formalidades y requisitos exigidos por las leyes y reglamentos, con eficacia por sí solos o en unión de otros complementarios para originar una inscripcíon o anotación.

ARTICULO 10.- El Registrador podrá exigir para formar o completar cada expediente o legajo una copia simple autorizada del documento que origine una inscripción o anotación.

ARTICULO 11.- Los documentos susceptibles de inscripción y anotación en el Registro son:

a) Escrituras públicas, entre ellas las que recojan los convenios de asociación y los estatutos de las empresas mixtas, así como sus modificaciones;

b) los contratos de asociación que instrumenten otras formas de asociación económica, así como sus modificaciones;

c) documentos expedidos por funcionarios administrativos, entre ellos la autorización de creación de la asociación económica de que se trate, que emitirá la Comisión referida en el Artículo 1 del Decreto-Ley 50;

d) documentos expedidos por funcionarios judiciales;

e) documentos privados.

ARTICULO 12.- La inscripción de las escrituras de constitución de empresas mixtas autorizadas por el Decreto-Ley 50 bajo la forma de compañias anónimas por acciones nominativas deberán expresar las circunstacias siguientes:

a) La denominación de la empresa, que seá adecuada al objeto de la misma según el Artículo 152 del Código de Comercio;

b) la expresión de que es sociedad anónima (S.A.);

c) domicilio de la empresa, con expresión de la calle y número y, si no hubiera número, con expresión de las calles que limiten la manzana;

d) especificación de las sucursales que tuviere establecidas;

e) nombre, apellidos, país de nacimiento, ciudadanía, edad, estado civil y domicilio de los otorgantes de la escritura social;, y, en su caso, el carácter y representación que ostenten con referencia a los apoderamientos que ejerzan;

f) el objeto social a que destinará su capital;

g) el capital social autorizado, con expresión del valor que se haya dado a los bienes aportados que no sea metálico y de las bases según las cuales se haya hecho el avalúo;

h) el número y valor nominal de las acciones en que el capital social estuviere dividido y representado, con expreción de las que hubiesen sido suscritas y de las que la sociedad conserva en cartera. Asimismo, se harán constar las emisiones autorizadas de acciones, expresando su valor nominal y condiciones y serie o series;

i) importe del capital suscrito y pagado al constituirse la empresa y plazos y modos en que habrá de desembolsarse el resto; y quiénes quedan autorizados para determinar el tiempo y modo en que hayan de satisfacerse los dividendos pasivos o ponerse en circulación las acciones que quedasen en cartera;

j) la duración de la empresa;

k) organización y atribuciones de la junta de accionistas;

l) el quórum requerido tanto para celebrar junta como para adoptar acuerdo y los requisitos que se exijan para el ejercicio del derecho de voto en la junta de accionistas;

m) la estructura y las atribuciones de la junta de directores;

n) el método mediante el cual adoptan sus decisiones la junta de accionistas y la junta de directores;

o) el nombramiento, atribuciones y responsabilidad de los funcionarios de la gerencia de la empresa;

p) los casos de disolución y el procedimiento para liquidar la empresa;

q) los demás pactos contenidos en el convenio de asociación, y

r) otras disposiciones de los estatutos orgánicos de la empresa.

ARTICULO 13.- A fin de cumplimentar su inscripción en el Registro, la reducción del capital social y de los demás actos modificativos de las empresas mixtas se harán constar por escritura pública que protocolice la certificación del Secretario de la entidad que consigne haberse tomado el acuerdo de reducción o de modificación por la Junta General de Accionistas con los requisitos y formalidades previstos en el Artículo 168 del Código de Comercio.

ARTICULO 14.- La inscripción de los contratos de asociación que instrumentan las formas restantes de asociacíon económica y sus posteriores modificaciones, deberán expresar los pactos y condiciones convenidos y los requisitos que resulten aplicables y pertinentes entre los consignados en el Artículo 12 precedente.

ARTICULO 15.- Para que los documentos públicos otorgados en otro país surtan efecto en el Registro deberán estar legalizados y protocolizados en Cuba y acompañar el certificado consular acreditativo de que el documento original o la certificación están extendidos con arreglo a las leyes del país de su otorgamiento y reúnen los requisitos y formalidades extrínsecas que se exijen para ser considerados como documento público. También deberá acompañarse, a las escrituras de sociedad constituida conforme a las leyes extranjeras, un certificado expedido por el cónsul cubano en el que haga constar que la sociedad está constituida y autorizada con arreglo a las leyes del país respectivo, todo lo cual deberá ser juntamente protocolizado con la escritura.

ARTICULO 16.- Para que surtan efecto en el Registro las copias de documentos originales extranjeros, o de certificaciones expedidas directamente de los originales por funcionarios extranjeros, en que nno conste protocolizada la certificación del funcionario consular a que se refiere el artículo anterior, será preciso que se presenten acompañadas de un acta notarial donde se declare bajo juramento por quien pretenda utilizarlas, o por su representante legal, que las mismas son auténticas y ciertos los actos o contratos que contiene, y que responde ante terceros de los perjuicios que con ello se ocasionen si resultaren falsas.

ARTICULO 17.- Los documentos otorgados en el extranjero en idioma que no sea el español sólo podrán inscribirse después de ser oficialmente traducidos.

ARTICULO 18.- Las sentencias dictadas por tribunales extranjeros no podrán inscribirse hasta que el Tribunal Supremo Popular disponga su ejecución.

ARTICULO 19.- Para que se practiquen las inscripciones o anotaciones dispuestas por resolución judicial o adminsitrativa, deberán ordenarse en mandamiento que se expedirá y presentará en el Registro, por duplicado; quedando un ejemplar archivado en el expediente o legajo correspondiente, hállase practicado o no la operación dispuesta.

ARTICULO 20.- Todo documento a inscribir o anotar en el Registro deberá ser asentado previamente en el Libro Diario de Presentaciones.

ARTICULO 21.- Si el documento no pudiese ser inscrito, a juicio del Registrado, por contener defectos subsanables o insubsanables y el interesado no optare por retirarlo dentro de los diez días siguientes, se le pondrá la correspondiente nota, expresando los motivos de la suspensión o denegatoria de inscripción. Igual nota se extenderá al margen del asiento de presentación.

ARTICULO 22.- Los poderes generales y especiales, excluyendo los conferidos para pleitos, sus modificaciones, sustituciones, revocatorias y renuncias, se incribirán en virtud de las correspondientes escrituras, transcribiéndose las facultades y demás circunstancias consignadas en dichos documentos.

ARTICULO 23.- Las anotaciones dispuestas por los tribunales en virtud de demanda declaratoria de quiebra o suspensión de pagos, contendrán las circunstancias siguientes:

a) Nombre del tribunal que la hubiere decretado;

b) clase de juicio;

c) objeto y extensión de la anotación;

d) fecha de la resolución judicial y de la presentación del mandamiento en el Registro con expresión del tomo y folio del Diario;

e) número con que quede archivado uno de los duplicados del mandamiento;

f) fecha y firma.

ARTICULO 24.- Será competente para ordernar la cancelación de cualquier anotación, en virtud de resolución ejecutoria, el funcionario o autoridad que la haya mandado hacer o el que la haya sucedido legalmente en el concimiento del juicio o expediente en que se hubiera decretado.

ARTICULO 25.- Los errores en que se incurriere al practicar una inscripción deberán ser subsanados por el Registrador cuando se advirtieren. En todo asiento o nota referente a rectificación de error se pondrá la fecha en que se efectuó y la suscribirá el Registrado.

ARTICULO 26.- A instancia de parte interesada, se podrán

expedir certificaciones, que podrán ser:

a) Literales, de uno o varios asientos o inscripciones, los cuales serán transcritos integramente;

b) en relación con uno o varios asientos o inscripciones o con determinados extremos de éstos;

c) negativas, cuando no constaren en los libros del Registro los datos cuya certificación se solicite.

ARTICULO 27.- Las certificaciones deberán ser expedidas dentro de los cuatro días siguientes al de la presentación de la solicitud, a no ser que por su extensión o por algún impedimento legal o material no fuere posible, lo que se hará constar al pie de la certificación.

ARTICULO 28.- Si la inscripción respecto de la cual se solicitase certificación estuviese cancelada, se hará constar así expresamente, aunque no se le pidiere; y si se tratase de una asociación cuyo término social apareciese vencido y no prorrogado se hará constar este extremo.

ARTICULO 29.- Estarán sujetas al pago de honorarios al Registro, según tarifa anexa a esta Resolución, las anotaciones, inscripciones y cancelaciones que se practicaren y las certificaciones que se expidieren, salvo cuando se ordenen de oficio por autoridad competente.

PUBLIQUESE en la Gaceta Oficial de la República, para general conocimiento.

DADA en la Cámara de Comercio de la República de Cuba, en la Ciudad de La Habana, a los 15 días del mes de septiembre de 1982.

*José Miguel Díaz Mirabal*
*Presidente de la Cámara de*
*Comercio de la República de Cuba*

ANEXO

## TARIFA DE HONORARIOS
### -EN PESOS CUBANOS, SEGUN LAS TASAS DE CAMBIO OFICIALES DEL BANCO NACIONAL DE CUBA-

| | |
|---|---:|
| Asiento de presentación | $ 50,00 |
| Inscripción de empresas mixtas | 500,00 |
| Inscripción de contratos de asociación que instrumentan otras formas de asociación económica | 400,00 |
| Otras anotaciones o inscripciones | 100,00 |
| Cancelaciones, modificaciones, sustituciones o revocaciones | 100,00 |
| Certificación literal de un asiento de inscripción | 100,00 |
| Certificación en relación con determinados extremos de una inscripcíon | 50,00 |
| Certificación negativa | 50,00 |

# GACETA OFICIAL
## DE LA REPUBLICA DE CUBA

EXTRAORDINARIA          LA HABANA, 22 DE JUNIO DE 1982          AÑO LXXX

## RESOLUCION No. 22/83

POR CUANTO: El Decreto-Ley No. 50, de 15 de febrero de 1982, dispone en su artículo 26, inciso a) que las empresas mixtas son sujetos del impuesto sobre utilidades.

POR CUANTO: El artículo 13 del "Reglamento para la Determinación de las Utilidades de las Empresas Mixtas" puesto en vigor mediante la Resolución No. 52 dictada por el que resuelve con fecha 15 de septiembre de 1982, estableció los porcentajes anuales máximos de depreciación de los activos fijos de las empresas mixtas deducibles de los ingresos brutos obtenidos por dichas empresas.

POR CUANTO: El Instituto Nacional de Turismo ha planteado y este Comité ha entendido atendible, que en el caso de instalaciones turísticas, dado su régimen de explotación, la depreciación real de las edificaciones resulta superior a la de las edificaciones dedicadas a otras actividades, provocando, en la práctica, un incremento de la utilidad imponible, por lo que resulta necesario modificar los porcentajes anuales máximos de depreciación de las edificaciones dedicadas a la actividad de turismo.

POR TANTO: En uso de las facualtades que me están conferidas,

**R e s u e l v o**:

PRIMERO: Modificar el inciso a) del Grupo I del artículo 13 del "Reglamento para la Determinación de las Utilidades de las Empresas Mixtas"; el que quedará redactado de la forma siguiente:

I  Edificaciones

a)Edificaciones de madera solamente,

| | |
|---|---|
| dedicadas a la explotación de la industria turística | 8% |
| de madera solamente, dedicadas a otras actividades | 6% |
| de mampostería y otros materiales, dedicadas a la explotación de la industria turística | 4% |
| de mampostería y otros materiales, dedicadas a otras actividades | 3% |

SEGUNDO: Publíquese en la Gaceta Oficial de la República para general conocimiento y archívese el original en la Dirección de Asesoría Jurídica de este Comité.

Dada en la Ciudad de La Habana, a los cinco días del mes de mayo de mil novecientos ochenta y tres.

*Francisco García Valls*
*Ministro-Presidente*
*Comité Estatal de Finanzas*

---

## RESOLUCION No. 23/83

POR CUANTO: El artículo 26 del Decreto Ley No. 50, de 15 de febrero de 1982, en su inciso a) dispone que las empresas mixtas y las partes en otras formas de asociación económica en los casos procedentes, son sujetos del impuesto sobre utilidades.

POR CUANTO: La Resolución No. 52, de fecha 15 de septiembre de 1982, de este Comité estableció: el "Reglamento para la Determinación de las Utilidades de las Empresas Mixtas"; las "Normas para el Pago del Impuesto sobre Ingresos de los Trabajadores (Impuesto sobre Nóminas) por las Empresas Mixtas"; y, las "Normas Relativas a la Obligatoriedad de Pagar el Recargo por MOra" establecido por el artículo 27 de la Ley No. 1213, de 27 de junio de 1967.

POR CUANTO: La Resolucicón No. 53, de fecha 15 de septiembre de 1962, de este Comité estableció las normas para la formación, utilización y liquidación, por parte de las empresas mixtas, de las reservas obligatorias para cubrir las contingencias que pudieran producirse en sus operaciones, así como otras reservas de carácter voluntario.

POR CUANTO: Las asociaciones económicas que no signifiquen la creación de empresas mixtas pero que tiene como objeto llevar a cabo la operación en conjunto por una entidad nacional y otra extranjera de instalaciones, plantas o fábricas operadas hasta entonces por la entidad nacional, revisten las mismas características que las empresas mixtas; por lo que resulta procedente hacer extensivas a las referidas asociaciones económicas las disposiciones mencionadas en los Por Cuantos anteriores.

POR TANTO: En uso de las facultades que me están conferidas,

## R e s u e l v o:

PRIMERO: Las partes que según el Decreto Ley No. 50, de 15 de febrero de 1982 constituyan en el territorio nacional asociaciones económicas que aún cuando no impliqluen la creación de una empresa mixta, tienen como objeto llevar a cabo operaciones en conjunto por una entidad nacional y otra extranjera de instalaciones, plantas o fábricas operadas hasta entonces por la entidad nacional, están obligadas a la observancia, y les son de aplicación las disposiciones contenidas en las siguientes Resoluciones de este Comité Estatal de Finanzas:

- Resolución No 52, de 15 de septiembre de 1982, sobre el "Reglamento para la Determinación de las Utilidades de las Empresas Mixtas"; "Las Normas para el Pago del Impuesto sobre Ingreso de los

Trabajadores (Impuesto sobre Nóminas)" y las "Normas Relativas a la Obligación de Pagar el Recargo por Mora".

- Resolución No. 53, de 15 de septiembre de 1982, sobre normas para la formación, utilización y liquidación de las reservas obligatorias para contingencias y otras reservas de carácter voluntario.

SEGUNDO: Las empresas estatales y organizaciones nacionales cubanas que suscriban los contratos de asociación a que se refiere la presente Resolución, quedan responsabilizadas con el pago de los impuestos y de cumplir las normas para la formación, utilización y liquidación de las reservas que se establecen en el apartado anterior de esta Resolución. Para ello incluirán en los contratos de asociación que suscriban con la parte extranjera los mecanismos para la retención de las cantidades correspondientes a los impuestos a liquidar y todo lo referente a la formación, utilización y liquidación de las reservas obligatorias para contingencias y otras reservas de carácter voluntario.

TERCERO: Publíquese en la Gaceta Oficial de la República para general conocimiento y archívese el original en la Dirección de Asesoría Jurídica de este Comité.

Dada en la Ciudad de La Habana, a los cinco días del mes de mayo de mil novecientos ochenta y tres.

*Francisco García Valls*
*Ministro-Presidente*
*Comité Estatal de Finanzas*

---

## RESOLUCION No. 24/83

POR CUANTO: El artículo 30 del Decreto-Ley No. 50, de 15 de febrero de 1982, establece que las partes en asociaciones económicas entre entidades cubanas y extranjeras, pueden determinar libremente el sistema de contabilidad más coveniente a los fines de la asociacíon económica, siempre qee el sistema adoptado se ajuste a los principios que universalmente se aceptan en este campo y que permite satisfacer las exigencias fiscales.

POR CUANTO: La Resolución No. 71, de fecha 26 de diciembre de 1976, de este Comité puso en vigor los Manuales del Sistema Nacional de Contabilidad y dispuso que todas las operaciones contables de los órganos y organismos del Estado y sus dependencias, así como las empresas estatales se realicen de conformidad y con la observancia de los métodos y sistemas a que se refieren los expresados manuales.

POR CUANTO: Las empresas estatales y otras organizaciones nacionales que se unan en asociación económica con intereses extranjeros que no signifique la creación de una persona jurídica, deben quedar exceptuadas de la obligación de aplicar las disposiciones a que se refiere el Por Cuanto anterior; por lo que se hace necesario dictar las normas al efecto.

POR TANTO: En uso de las facultades qué me están conferidas.

## R e s u e l v o:

PRIMERO: Exceptuar de la obligación de aplicar los Manuales del Sistema Nacional de contabilidad titulados "Sistema Nacional de Contabilidad para Unidades Presupuestadas" y "Sistema Nacional de Contabilidad para las Empresas" y por consiguiente de la obligación de realizar sus operaciones contables de conformidad y con la observancia de los métodos y sistemas a que se contraen dichos manuales, a las empresas estatales y a cualesquiera otras organizaciones nacionales que se unan en asociación económica que no constituyan empresas mixtas con intereses extranjeros dentro del territorio nacional, durante todo el período de vigencia de la asociación referida, en lo que respecta a las operaciones en dicha asociación.

SEGUNDO: Las empresas estatales y cualesquiera otras organizaciones nacionales que se unan en asociación económica que no constituyan empresas mxitas con intereses extranjeros dentro de territorio nacional realizarán sus operaciones contables en lo que respecta a dicha asociación, de conformidad y con la observancia de los métodos y sistemas que se determinen en los contratos de asociación.

TERCERO: Publíquese en la Gaceta Oficial de la República para general conocimiento y archívese el orignal en la Dirección de Asesoría Jurídica de este Comité.

DADA en la Ciudad de La Habana, a los cinco días del mes de mayo de mil novecientos ochenta y tres.

*Francisco García Valls*
*Ministro-Presidente*
*Comité Estatal de Finanzas*

# GACETA OFICIAL

## DE LA REPUBLICA DE CUBA

EXTRAORDINARIA    LA HABANA, JUEVES 23 DE JUNIO DE 1983    AÑO LXXXI

Imprenta: Zanja No. 352, esq. a Escobar. - Habana 2

Número 42                                                                 Página 627

## COMITES ESTATALES

---

### ESTADISTICAS
### RESOLUCION No. 96/83

POR CUANTO: El Consejo de Estado ha autorizado mediante el Decreto Ley No. 50 del 15 de febrero de 1982, la creación de asociaciones económicas entre entidades cubanas y extranjeras.

POR CUANTO: Es atribución del Comité Estatal de Estadísticas la captación y el procesamiento de la información comprendida en el Sistema de Información Estadística Nacional.

POR TANTO: En uso de las facultades que me están conferidas,

### R e s u e l v o:

PRIMERO: La información estadística fundamental requerida sobre las actividades de las asociaciones económicas autorizadas por el Decreto Ley No. 50 de 1982, será la siguiente:

a) La información contenida en los estados financiaros establecido para este tipo de asociación económica.

b) Información sobre la Fuerza de Trabajo, en su caso.

c) Otras informaciones específicas de acuerdo a la actividad de que se trate, fundamentalmente las referidas, a la producción, exportaciones e importaciones, tanto de bienes como de servicios.

SEGUNDO: Las informaciones estadísticas señaladas en los incisos a) y b) del Apartado anterior se obtendrán, respectivamente, a través del Comité Estatal de Finanzas y la empresa cubana empleadora.

TERCERO: Las informaciones específicas a que se refiere el inciso c) del Apartado anterior se suministrarán directamente a este Comité Estatal de Estadísticas por las asociaciones económicas.

CUARTO: La Dirección de Finanzas, Costos y Precios del Comité Estatal de Estadísticas será la encargada de coordinar y definir con las asociaciones económicas la información estadística necesaria de acuerdo con la actividad que éstas desarrollan y definirá las formas de entrega y flujo de dicha información.

QUINTO: Las Direcciones que atienden Sectores y Categorias Globales del Comite Estatal de Estadísticas presentarán a la Dirección de Finanzas, Costos y Precios del propio Comité, la selección de indicadores correspondientes a su esfera de atención.

SEXTO: La Cámara de Comercio de la República de Cuba, una vez inscrita la asociación económica en su registros, informará a la Dirección de Metodología del Comite Estatal de Estadisticas, su constitución, a fin de efectuar el registro y asignar el código que le corresponda para su identificación númerica de acuerdo con la atividad económica que desarrolle y en función de los Clasificadores vigentes en el país.

SEPTIMO: Notifíquese la presente Resolución a los Vicepresidentes, Jefes de las Unidades Organizativas Mayores del Comité Estatal de Estadísticas y a cuantas más personas naturales y jurídica proceda.

DADA, en el Comité Estatal de Estadísticas, en la Ciudad de La Habana, a los seis días del mes de mayo de mil novecientos ochenta y tres.

*Fidel Vascós González*
*Ministro-Presidente*
*Comité Estatal de Estadísticas*

# GACETA OFICIAL

## DE LA REPUBLICA DE CUBA

EXTRAORDINARIA    LA HABANA, LUNES 4 DE JULIO DE 1983    AÑO LXXXI

Imprenta: Zanja No. 352, esq. a Escobar. - Habana 2

Número 16

Página 127

## CONSEJO DE ESTADO

FIDEL CASTRO RUZ, **Presidente del Consejo de Estado de la República de Cuba.**

HAGO SABER: Que el Consejo de Estado, en uso de las facultades que le han sido conferidas, ha aprobado lo siguiente:

POR CUANTO: El Artículo 35 del Decreto-Ley Número 50, de 15 de febrero de 1982 dispone que "las empresas mixtas, y las partes de las demás formas de asociación económica, son sujetos de los contratos económicos definidos en el Decreto-Ley Número 15, de 3 de julio de 1978, cuya concertación y ejecución se rigen por la legislación económica vigente"; pero es lo cierto que la participación de una empresa mixta o de una parte en las demás formas de asociación económica con intereses extranjeros obliga a dictar condiciones especiales de contratación, facultad que corresponde al Consejo de Ministros según la Disposición Especial Primera del Decreto-Ley Número 15, de 1978.

POR CUANTO: El Artículo 3 del Decreto-Ley Número 50, de 15 de febreo de 1982 dispone que la Comisión creada por el Comité Ejecutivo del Consejo de Ministros al amparo del Artículo 1 del expresado Decreto-Ley Número 50, establecerá las condiciones a que deberán someterse las empresas mixtas y demás asociaciones económicas.

POR TANTO: El Consejo de Estado, en uso de las atribuciones que le están conferidas en el inciso c) del Artículo 83 de la Constitución de la República, resuelve dictar el siguiente:

# DECRETO-LEY NUMBERO 71

ARTICULO 1.- La Comisión creada al amparo de lo dispuesto en el Artículo 1 del Decreto-Ley Númbero 50, de 15 de febrero de 1982, regulará las condiciones a que se someterán las relaciones económicas contractuales en que participen dentro del territorio nacional las empresas mixtas o las partes en las demás formas de asociación, hasta tanto el Consejo de Ministros dicte las condiciones especiales de los contratos económicos correspondientes.

ARTICULO 2.- Los conflictos entre las empresas mixtas y las partes en las demás formas de asociación económica con las empresas estatales y otras organizaciones nacionales con motivo de la ejecución de contratos económicos serán resueltos por el Organo Nacional de Arbitraje Estatal.

## DISPOSICION FINAL

UNICA: Se derogan cuantas disposiciones legales y reglamentarias se opongan al cumplimiento de lo dispuesto en el presente Decreto-Ley, el que comenzará a regir a partir de su publicación en la Gaceta Oficial de la República.

DADO, en el Palacio de la Revolucíón en la Ciudad de La Habana, a los cuatro días del mes de julio de mil novecientos ochenta y tres.

*Fidel Castro Ruz*

## GACETA OFICIAL 26 de agosto de 1989
## BANCO NACIONAL DE CUBA
### RESOLUCION NUMERO DOSCIENTOS
### VEINTINUEVE DE 1989

POR CUANTO: El Decreto-Ley No. 50, de 15 de febrero de 1982, Sobre Asociación Económica entre Entidades Cubanas y Extranjeras, establece en su Artículo 20 que se aplicarán las tasas de cambio oficiales del Banco Nacional de Cuba para: a) la valoración en moneda convertible de servicios, salarios y otras prestaciones cuando se cobren sobre la base de tarifas expresadas en moneda naciona; b) la conversión de los impuestos y otras obligaciones fiscales cuyo importe se expresa en moneda nacional; c) cualquier otro canje de moneda.

POR CUANTO: El Decreto-Ley No. 84 de 13 de octubre de 1984 en su Artículo 36 inciso 26, establece entre las funciones del Banco NaCIonal de Cuba, la de fijar el tipo de cambio de peso cubano en relación con otras monedas extranajeras.

POR CUANTO: Conviene dejar establecidas las bases de los tipos de cambio oficiales del Banco Nacional de Cuba a ser aplicados a las transacciones de las empresas mixtas y las partes de otras formas de asociación económica a que se refiere el Decreto-Ley No. 50.

POR CUANTO: Corresponde al Ministro Presidente del Banco Nacional de Cuba dictar resoluciones, instrucciones y demás disposiciones necesarias para la ejecución de las funciones del Banco Nacional de Cuba, de carácter obligatorio para todos los órganos, organismos, empresas y otras entidades económicas estatales, cooperativas, organizaciones y asociaciones económicas, el sector privado y la población; según lo establecido en el Artículo 52 inciso a) del antes citado Decreto Ley No. 84.

POR CUANTO: El que resuelve fue nombrado Presidente del Banco Nacional de Cuba por acuerdo del Consejo de Estado de 5 de noviembre de 1985, el que fue ratificado mediante acuerdo de la Asamblea Nacional del Poder Popular de 27 de diciembre del mismo año.

POR TANTO: En uso de las atribuciones que me han sido conferidas:

# R e s u e l v o:

PRIMERO: Los tipos de cambio aplicables a las transacciones de las empresas mixtas y las partes de las otras formas de asociación económica a que se refiere el Decreto-Ley No. 50 de 15 de febrero de 1982, se basarán en la paridad uno a uno (1:1) del peso cubano con el dólar estadounidense y reflejarán diariamente, mediante la tasa cruzada, las cotizaciones del mercado de New York para el resto de las monedas libremente convertibles.

SEGUNDO: De acuerdo con lo establecido en el apartado anterior, los tipos de cambio aplicables a las transacciones de las empresas mixtas y las partes de otras formas de asociación económica serán los tipos de cambio oficales que emite diariamente el Banco Nacional de Cuba para los Certificados de Divisas y que se publican en la prensa nacional, debiendo considerarse en todos los casos el tipo de cambio que aparece en la columna denominada "Canjes" en la fecha en que se efectúe la transacción.

TERCERO: El régimen contemplado en los apartados primero y segundo de la presente Resolucón se aplicará exclusivamente a las transacciones que realicen tanto las empresas mixtas en su condición de persona jurídica, así como las partes de otras formas de asociación económica a que se refiere el Decreto-Ley No. 50. Dicho régimen no será aplicado a los ciudadanos extranjeros no residentes y residentes temporales que laboren en las referidas asociaciones económicas, con relación a los cuales se continuarán aplicando las regulaciones establecidas por el Banco Nacional de Cuba para estos casos.

COMUNIQUESE: A los Vicepresidentes del Banco Nacional de Cuba, al Banco Financiero Internacional, a los Organismos de la Administración Central del Estado y archívese el original en Secretaría.

PUBLIQUESE en la Gaceta Oficial de la República para su conocimiento general.

Ciudad de La Habana, 22 de julio de 1989.

*Héctor Rodríguez Llompart*
*Ministro Presidente*
*Banco Nacional de Cuba*

# CURRENT INVESTMENTS IN CUBA

**Table I. PARTIAL LIST OF FOREIGN JOINT VENTURES WITH CUBAN PARTNERS**

| Foreign entity | Cuban entity | Project | Status | Value of Foreign Investment | Comments |
|---|---|---|---|---|---|
| **Brazil** | | | | | |
| SM Diesel | | Manufacture of meningitis-B vaccine | Signed in 1991 | $50 million | Manufacturing to take place in Brazil |
| **Canada** | | | | | |
| Emery International | Cubanacán | Tourism (refurbishing of buses) | Approved in 1991 | | JV called Caribbean Diesel, S.A. Buses to be used by tourists. |
| | | Biodegradable egg trays | | | |
| **Chile** | | | | | |
| Santa Ana/ Latinexim | | Tourism | | | Food for international tourism industry |
| Carlos Cardoen | | Shoe manufacturing | | | Footwear for export and sale in dollar stores |
| **Curaçao** | | | | | |
| Curaçao Dry Dock | Astillero Casablanca | Ship repair | Signed 1991 | | Ship repair in Curaçao. Pending approval by Curaçao Island Council. |
| **Finland** | | | | | |
| | Cubanacán | Tourism | Signed 1990 | | Build hotel and 50 cabanas in Santiago de Cuba |
| **India** | | | | | |
| Cimmco International | | Textiles production | Expected to be Signed 1991 | | JV with Santa Clara textile mill. |
| **Ireland** | | | | | |
| Aer Rianta | Cubanacán | Tourism (airport management and aircraft maintenance) | | | |
| **Italy** | | | | | |
| Italcable, S.A. | Ministerio de Comunicaciones | International communications | | $35-$50 million | JV will replace enterprise Intertel. |
| Benetton | Cubanacán | Tourism (8 stores for tourists) | First store opened in 1993 | | Also participating is Connolly, a Bahamas-based corporation owned by Benetton |

| Company | Cuban partner | Product | Date | Value | Notes |
|---|---|---|---|---|---|
| **Jamaica** | | | | | |
| Super Clubs | Cubanacán | Tourism | Signed 1990 | | Expansion of Villa Los Cactos Hotel, Varadero. New construction, Cuba-Cuba Hotel, Varadero. |
| **Lithuania** | | | | | |
| | | Electricity meters | Started November 1991 | | JV called Teven, S.A. |
| **Mexico** | | | | | |
| Various Monterrey businessmen | | Cotton fabric and apparel | Signed October 1992 | $50 million; up to $611 million | JV called International Textile Corporation (ITC) |
| **Spain** | | | | | |
| Mármoles de San Marino | Empresa Nacional de Mármoles | Marble | Signed October 1991 | | JV called Marmolex, S.A. |
| Unidiamond | Empresa Nacional de Mármoles | Production of disks to cut marble | Signed October 1991 | | JV called Cardiamond, S.A. |
| Española Miesa, S.A. | Tecenergo | Energy-saving projects | Signed November 1991 | $150,000 | JV called Cuvastec. |
| Asturcoex | Emidict (Academia de Ciencias) | Laser medical equipment | Signed November 1991 | | JV called Tece, S.A. |
| Asturcoex | Emidict (Academia de Ciencias) | Industrial Systems | Signed | November 1991 | |
| Esfera 2000 | Cubanacán | Tourism | | | JV called Turni, S.A. Build Tuxpán Hotel in Varadero. |
| Grupo Sol | Cubanacán | Tourism | Signed 1987 or 1988 | $150 million | Build Sol Palmeras and Meliá Varadero Hotels; 3 others planned. |
| Ibercusa | Cubanacán | Tourism | Signed in 1988 or 1989 | | Build Cohiba Hotel, Havana. JV called Hocusa. |
| Oasis Corporation | Cubanacán | Tourism | | | Build a 1920 Hotel in Varadero; build facilities in Cayo Largo. |
| Grupo Havana | Cubanacán | Tourism | Started May 1991 | $1 million | Discotheque in Comodoro Hotel, Havana. JV called Havana Club. |
| Gruexva | Cubanacán | Tourism | Signed November 1991 | $120 million over 8 years | Build 3250-room complex in Isle of Youth. JV called Cuvasa. |
| **Switzerland** | | | | | |
| Suidol | | Tourism | Signed 1988 or '89 | | Build a 40-yacht marina in Jucaro. |
| **United Kingdom** | | | | | |
| Technical and Manufacturing Services | Quimimport | Chemical cleanser | | | Debt-for-equity swap. |

Sources: Information culled from various issues of *Cuba Business* and from other trade journals and newspapers.

**Table II. OTHER ARRANGEMENTS WITH FOREIGN ENTITIES**

| Foreign entity | Cuban entity | Project | Status | Comments |
| --- | --- | --- | --- | --- |
| **Chile** | | | | |
| Agrícola Las Araucarias and Oceánica Chilena | | Technology for marketing fruits and vegetables | | Marketing agreement |
| New World Fruit | Ministerio de Agricultura | Marketing of citrus fruits | | Marketing agreement. Sale into Western Europe. New World is located in Rotterdam. |
| **France** | | | | |
| Maestra Energía Pompes Guinard | Energoimport | Assembly of electric generators Assembly of deep well pumps | | Cooperative processing. Pumps assembled at the Planta Mecánica, Santa Clara. |
| **Italy** | | | | |
| San Marco Inter-Canada | Profiel | Furniture | | Cooperative processing. San Marco will provide Canadian hides. |
| San Marco Inter-Canada Fiatallis | Profiel | Furniture (minibars) Fork Lifts | Signed 1989 | |
| **Mexico** | | Soap and detergent production | | |
| **Netherlands** | | | | |
| Castrol-Holanda | ECIMACT | Production of lubricants | Agreement signed February 1983 | |

| Foreign entity | Cuban entity | Project | Status | Comments |
|---|---|---|---|---|
| **Spain** | | | | |
| Creaciones Meta | Profiel | Wooden toys | | Cooperative processing. |
| Girabu | | Assembly of washing machines | | Cooperative processing. |
| Industria Sevillana de Automoción | | Assembly of transmission systems | Signed 1988 | Cooperative processing. |
| ENASA | Transimport and truck factory "Narciso López Roselló" | Assembly of light trucks | | |
| Lebrero | | Assembly of ground compactor | Signed 1989 | |
| Grupo Barreiro/Pegaso | | Assembly of Taino EB V8 gasoline engines | | |
| Pegaso | | Assembly of buses | | |
| M.Z. Imer | | Assembly of cement mixer | | |
| Betico | | Assembly of portable compressor | | |
| **USSR** | | Assembly of apparel and footwear | Signed April 1989 | Cooperative processing. |
| **Venezuela** | | | | |
| Corporación Regional del Sudoeste | Ministerio de la Industria Básica | Fertilizer production | Probably signed 1992 | Third country association. Will use Venezuelan phosphates and Cuban nitrogenizing technology. |

Sources: Information culled from various issues of *Cuba Foreign Trade*, *Cuba Business*, and from other trade journals and newspapers.

## Table III. NUMBER OF CUBAN JOINT VENTURES WITH FOREIGN INVESTORS

| Date | Number of Joint Ventures | | | Cuban Source |
|---|---|---|---|---|
| | Concluded | Under Discussion | Total | |
| December 1990 | | | 20 | Chamber of Commerce |
| April 1991 | 55 | 100 | 155 | J. Garcia Oliveras, Chamber of Commerce |
| June 1991 | | | 70 | J. Garcia Oliveras, Chamber of commerce |
| July 1991 | 40 | 110 | 150 | J. Garcia Oliveras, Chamber of Commerce |
| October 1991 | 50 | 100 | 150 | Chamber of Commerce |
| December 1991a | 50+ | 140 | 190+ | J. Garcia Oliveras, Chamber of Commerce |
| December 1991b | 60 | 150 | 210 | J. Garcia Oliveras, Chamber of Commerce |
| March 1992 | 200 | 150 | 350 | H. Rodríguez Llompart, Cuban National Bank |
| June 1992a | 60 | 100 | 160 | O. Alfonso Montalvan, State Committee for Economic Cooperation |
| June 1992b | 250 | several thousand | several thousand | C. Lage, Politburo member |
| November 1992 | 76 | | | |

Sources: December 1990—*Cuba Business*, no.6 (December 1990), p.11.; April 1991—Whitefield (1991b).; June 1991—Whitefield (1991a); July 1991—Main (1991); October 1991—Cuba Aggressively (1991:4A).; December 1991a—Jenkins (1991:11A).; December 1991b—*Cuba Business*, no.6 (December 1991),p.15.; March 1992—Business International (1992:24).; June 1992a—Sevcec (1992:5A).; June 1992b—Thurston (1992:10A); November 1992—Carlos Lage (1992:8).
These tables were provided courtesy of Jorge Pérez López, ed. *Cuba at the Crossroads.* (Gainesville: University of Florida Press, 1994).